LESSONS TO LAST: AN INFORMAL GUIDE TO SURVIVING AND THRIVING IN TEACHING

by John A. Welsman

Copyright © 2024 John Andrew Welsman

All rights reserved. No part or portion of this book may be reproduced in any form without permission from the author and/or publisher, except as permitted by U.S. copyright law. For permissions, contact jandrewwelsman@gmail.com

JOHN A WELSMAN

Foreword

Firstly, hello! Or as we say in my corner of the world, Aotearoa New Zealand, *Kia Ora*! If you have picked up this book, there is a good chance that you are a teacher or considering training to be one. I'm a high school teacher myself; though I love my job, something has been worrying me recently—too many good teachers are leaving the classroom. By some estimates, close to 50% of new teachers leave the profession within their first five years. That's not good for students, schools, communities, or the teachers themselves who invest their time and money to train. So why have I been fortunate enough to find myself teaching after more than a decade on the job? Upon reflection, the reason is straightforward; it's only because other teachers had offered me support or advice when I was starting out in the profession. That made me wonder—if I could rewind the clock and hand myself a book containing all of the lessons, strategies, and habits that I have picked up along the way, what would that look like? Most importantly, would such a book have made my first few years a little less stressful?

This is the book that resulted from that question. It contains the lessons I wish I had learned BEFORE I found myself in a classroom. In sharing them, I hope I can help you avoid many of the pitfalls faced by new teachers and thereby reduce your day-to-day stress, better manage your workload, and build a dynamic and fulfilling career in education.

This is not an academic text. There are no references and no footnotes; just reflections and anecdotes to illustrate what I believe are the most important and useful principles of education design, delivery, and classroom and career management based on my experiences in high school classrooms and by observing some great teachers in action. The opinions herein are mine and do not represent those of any employer, past or present. Names are fictional and the scenarios described are instructive examples based on real-life experiences. It is my sincere hope this book will help you in your journey to becoming the teacher you want to be and that your students deserve.

LESSONS TO LAST

TABLE OF CONTENTS

Introduction: Why Do You Want to Teach?

Section 1: Preparation for Teaching

    Lesson 1: Accept the absurdity

    Lesson 2: Names are powerful

    Lesson 3: Teach as if you're telling a story

    Lesson 4: Don't reinvent the wheel

    Lesson 5: Fill the pool before swimming

    Lesson 6: Respect the room

Section 2: Life in the classroom

    Lesson 7: Set simple expectations

    Lesson 8: Communicate proactively

    Lesson 9: Be future-focused when writing report cards

    Lesson 10: Get angry before you get angry

    Lesson 11: Don't be too nice

    Lesson 12: Natural justice is the goal

    Lesson 13: Kids are fairness detectors

    Lesson 14: Your voice is your most valuable tool

    Lesson 15: "Gamify" everything

    Lesson 16: Build relationships outside the classroom

    Lesson 17: Optimism has no place in planning field trips

    Lesson 18: Everyone in the school contributes to success

    Lesson 19: Recognize the rightful limits of your influence

Lesson 20: Develop micro-habits to go the distance

Section 3: Managing and optimizing your career

Lesson 21: Pay your bills on time

Lesson 22: Trouble is often the consequence of seemingly small decisions

Lesson 23: Be deliberate about where you work and what you teach

Lesson 24: Interviews are like first dates

Lesson 25: Don't get cocky!

Conclusion

INTRODUCTION: WHY DO YOU WANT TO TEACH?

Some people have had a desire to teach from an early age. Or perhaps you find yourself in a tough job market or have been laid off during the pandemic. Maybe you find yourself mid-career and looking for a change. Either way, you need to make a living, and teaching *can* be a rewarding way of doing it.

Many teacher education programs require that you have done some volunteer work in the classroom. I would highly recommend that you do this in the first instance, as it gives you some perspective on the job before diving in. I think you will find most schools will be quite willing to engage with volunteers given the general shortage of teachers in many places (note that a well-run school will conduct a police-check on you first). Volunteering also gives school administrators a chance to "check you out" well before the formal interviewing stage. During my undergraduate degree, I volunteered for a number of hours at a primary school in my neighborhood. At first, I was a fly-on-the-wall observing how things were run, although as time went on the classroom teacher had me assist some students with their reading, which I found quite rewarding. Given the investment in time and money that is involved with a teacher education program, I would suggest you try it out as a volunteer before you begin.

Some people are apt to say that teachers are born, rather than made. Although it helps for a teacher to have certain personality traits, I believe that just about anyone can be effective in the job if they find their niche (and as I will explain later, job and school *fit* is critically important in this regard). So, whether you are just starting university/college, finishing up an apprenticeship, or thinking about a change of job, teaching *is* worth considering.

The advantages and challenges

Despite the cultural, social, and economic differences in school structures and philosophies of education worldwide, teaching as a profession is defined by remarkably similar rewards and challenges. As a teacher, you will have the privilege of influencing the choices and paths your students will take. Ideally, your influence will also make the journey of adolescence a little more tolerable than it might otherwise be for some children (as many of us remember, adolescence is generally tough work). If you teach for any number of years, you will get to know and influence potentially thousands of people during their progression to adulthood. Some of those people *will* remember you. Don't be surprised if you bump into a former student on the street or in a store and they excitedly tell you what they have been up to and what they are planning to do in the future. In my view, these encounters are one of the very best rewards of the job. Incidentally, conversations like this may also be one of the best indicators that you have been effective in your job. Overall, if you enjoy working with young people and helping them to navigate their life choices, teaching could be a good fit for you.

You might also have a fair amount of autonomy in how you do your job (albeit within the constraints of the curriculum and school structure). I say this as a teacher working in New Zealand, a country that is known for having a curriculum that gives teachers significant latitude in formulating courses and learning programs tailored to its diverse communities. Admittedly, you may not have this degree of freedom in all places. Regardless of where you teach, if you enjoy creating interesting ways of communicating your passions (whether it be languages, mathematics, science, etc.) and adopting the perspectives of other people while doing so, then teaching may be a good choice for you. When it's going well, the hours and days will fly by and you will never look at the clock out of boredom.

Job Security

One of the big benefits of teaching is job security. If you work in a public school, the government will generally have to implode for you to go unpaid. Compared to work in the private sector, you will also be more insulated from the vagaries of global economics in terms of bringing home a pay cheque. Furthermore, It is probably fair to say that you won't be subject to the same risk of summary dismissal or layoffs as you might be in the corporate world.

Teaching is also a relatively mobile career, in many cases allowing you to move between towns and regions more easily than in other jobs. After all, in almost every town there is a school. Another benefit of teaching is that employers in other sectors generally recognize that people who have worked as teachers can work within tight deadlines, manage a workload, and can be trusted with things (such as the care of small humans); so, consider that a plus too. Teachers also tend to have well-developed "soft skills" useful in communicating, relating, and resolving conflict in today's increasingly social work environments. In addition, a teacher's ability to work productively with people from all backgrounds is a highly sought-after skill set in the modern economy. Overall, employers recognize that teachers tend to be well-adjusted, socially adept team players.

On Money

Let's be upfront about this—nobody goes into teaching expecting to get rich. In the United States of America, there are huge variations in teacher salaries, with some locations paying low wages that are arguably criminal. Oddly enough, some politicians seem not to notice (or care) that teachers in such situations sometimes have had to resort to working part-time jobs in addition to teaching to make ends meet. Perhaps they see that as role-modeling the value of hard work for the kids! In contrast to the United States, some of the best-paid teachers work in places such as Singapore, Canada, Australia, and certain European countries. Well-qualified and experienced Canadian and Australian teachers can make six-figure salaries.

In terms of remuneration, teaching is not a highly scalable enterprise. Unlike professions such as medicine, law, or accounting, there aren't easily accessible options for practicing your trade in the context of a business and achieving the scalability of income associated with that path. Nevertheless, opportunities exist for teachers to transition to consulting or leverage their experience into other realms such as publishing, education software development, or government service after they have gained some credible experience in the classroom.

The scale of public education in many countries is extensive and this has a significant impact on salaries. There may be tens of thousands of people employed as teachers by local, state, or federal governments. If unionized, they will be bound by collective agreements on salaries and working conditions. One of the outcomes of this large-scale collective bargaining is that pay increases can balloon government budgets very quickly depending on the number of people employed in the sector. As a consequence, approving across-the-board increases to tens of thousands of workers such as teachers can be a difficult proposition for a government attempting to balance the competing demands for public funds in challenging economic times.

The Hours

To be effective at teaching, you will have to put in the hours (and you won't get paid by the hour either). Both you (and the kids) will know if you don't. Although there may be some unicorns who can walk into the classroom, capture hearts and minds, obtain good exam results, *and* leave at the same time as the kids, I haven't come across them. In fact, I'm pretty sure they don't exist. Accept working after-hours and on the weekend, especially at the beginning of your career.

In my experience, at the outset of your teaching career the hours you put in balance out the "holiday" time you have off, putting you on par with most other jobs in terms of annual leave. In time, if you teach certain subjects (more on that later) and don't jump schools frequently, the overtime hours will decrease and the holiday time will go up. Therefore, this aspect is not a dealbreaker.

As a vocation, teaching can sometimes be subject to unreasonable societal expectations about what you can accomplish. Depending on where you are in the world, society may expect you to approach your work with unsustainable effort, tolerate low pay, expect you to compensate for years of parental and institutional neglect, undo the wrongs of history, and/or compel children to take on academic challenges which they may not need or are not suited for. People (both students and teachers) have limits. Expect the best—both *for* and *from*—everyone involved; but remember, attempt to be reasonable in terms of what you demand of yourself and others.

The disrepute clause

Implicit (or explicit) in many employment agreements is the disrepute clause, in which bringing your employer into disrepute can be a cause for dismissal. Teachers are especially subject to these considerations. Obviously, there are many jobs where this expectation applies, though there are many others where it does not. For some jobs, getting drunk in public and posting the experience to social media, though unwise, is unlikely to severely hinder your job prospects. That is not the case in teaching. What you say and do in public (and what you post online) can come back to you. As a teacher, you are expected to be a role model for children and so your conduct in and out of school must withstand the highest level of scrutiny. What I'm trying to say is that you will be held to a higher standard than the general population. Whether this is unfair is beyond the scope of this book; I'm merely conveying to you the societal expectation. Prepare to have your behavior scrutinized!

Having been forewarned and forearmed with the rewards and challenges of teaching, I hope you have chosen to take this path. There is quite literally no other job like it...

INTRODUCTION TO THE LESSONS

Consider this book as an aspirational guide. Being an effective teacher is a pursuit that never ends. When viewed retrospectively, you will be amazed at the progress you will make over the course of a few short years. Accept that the journey is a long and nebulous process and you will have made a good start on your path to becoming an effective teacher.

Teaching is a highly collegial vocation; you will succeed or fail based on the relationships you cultivate with your colleagues and how closely you observe the conduct, strategies, and practices of the most respected teachers in your school. In many ways, effective teaching is intellectual genealogy in practice; you tend to collect strategies, resources, tips and tricks from experienced colleagues and pass them on in turn over time. This book is formulated in that spirit; these are the lessons I have learned from successful teachers I have observed and worked with over the course of more than a decade in New Zealand schools. It also contains my personal observations and some of the refinements on these strategies that I have made during my time in the classroom. This is the book I wish I had been given when I was starting in the profession. I hope you find it useful.

SECTION 1: PREPARATION FOR TEACHING

One of the most important lessons I learned during my first year in the profession was that much of the work required for effective teaching happens before you step into the classroom. At the start of your career, your actual hours spent in the classroom will represent a small proportion of the time you will actually be "working". To be effective in the classroom, you will need to do the following:

a) Understand who you'll teach (i.e., know who your students are as individuals);
b) Know what to teach (and be deliberate about formulating units of work and lessons);
c) Prepare the classroom for teaching and learning (i.e., get the environment right);
d) Cultivate the mental space (i.e., set expectations for student learning and behavior), and;
e) Be prepared for the unexpected once you're in the classroom

With that said, we'll begin by examining why it's useful to adopt a "big picture" mindset when approaching the practice of teaching and learning in a modern school.

LESSON 1: ACCEPT THE ABSURDITY

I think the first step in enjoying your job as a teacher is to embrace the utter absurdity of your mission. When viewed objectively, modern systems of education represent a bizarre situation in comparison to how people have learned throughout much of history. Up until very recently, humans lived in small groups, interacting with a few or hundred-odd other individuals over the course of what were comparatively short lifetimes comprising a few decades at most. Children would learn by *doing* alongside other adults, often by being given responsibility at an early age for relatively important jobs such as food gathering, the growing of crops, or the care of livestock. When viewed from this historical vantage point, an objective observer would agree that segregating children by age and compartmentalizing their days into discrete chunks interrupted by periodic bells is decidedly *unnatural*. That this regimentation of behavior is compelled during the transition from childhood to young adulthood makes conventional models of schooling a decidedly drastic psychological departure from what was normal for much of human history. *In other words, don't be surprised if the kids sometimes misbehave at school.*

That being said, there are practical reasons why schools developed as they did. In almost all circumstances nowadays parents *need* to work, requiring the provision of de facto childcare by the state (i.e., the government) during "working" hours. Where the state has taken on this responsibility, it must provide this service at a reasonable cost, necessitating the staffing of schools with the minimum practical number of teachers. Even though modern systems of education are an awkward compromise from a psycho-social standpoint and far from perfect in their design and delivery, it is nevertheless recognized that public education is an undeniable social and economic good. Not only does education create the conditions for long-term economic growth through the development of intellectual and social capital (i.e., a literate and numerate citizenry), it also provides one of the best methods of intergenerational socio-economic mobility (which has benefits for everyone). These benefits and constraints, coupled with the broad influences of industrialization, have shaped education as we now know it.

Our lives have been improved in a number of ways by the provision of publicly funded schools. This is not to say that they are perfect—far from it. Schools represent a compromise between competing social aspirations, needs, and constraints. My point is that as a teacher, you can avoid considerable stress and self-doubt about your efficacy by acknowledging that many of the challenges of student behavior and learning are the product of the compromise represented by the idea of a "school". Your goal, if you are to survive (and thrive) in the job, is to work within these constraints. Accept that there will be days when "good enough" represents a job well done.

LESSON 2: NAMES ARE POWERFUL

The first step in becoming an effective teacher is to build good relationships with your students. Spend some time during the first day getting to know names; in fact, try to know your students' names before you step into the classroom on the first day. I'll be upfront; I'm not good at learning names. Although I would never forget a face, names have always been challenging (and I doubt I'm alone in this respect).

Why should learning student names be a priority? First, knowing and using a student's name shows that you care enough about them to remember their name. Second, it has been said (by a very talented teacher I admire) that *"names are power"* in the classroom. Classrooms can be busy, noisy places. Using directed instructions with a name can emphasize a point and make it more likely that an instruction is followed. In addition, a direct instruction with a name is a whole lot better than a vague "hey you!". Finally, people simply enjoy hearing their names spoken in conversation; it is psychologically gratifying.

During the first lesson with a new class, I will have students write a bit of an introduction to themselves, which involves a list of fill-in-the blank statements that they complete to give me a bit of an understanding of their background and interests. The list often looks something like this:

1) Today, I'm feeling...
2) Something I find easy...

3) Something I find challenging…
4) If I could do anything I want after high school, I would…
5) I spend most of my time with…
6) Something I bet my teacher doesn't know about me…

As students are completing this, I walk around the room and start a conversation about something they have written. As I'm doing so, I'll try to use their name. If I can't, I'll make it a bit of a game and ask for the first, second, or third letter until I get things right. The mental acrobatics involved in doing that, coupled with a conversation about the icebreaker they are writing, will often help to attach a name to a face. This approach to learning names is backed up by science; oddly enough, increasing the complexity of the circumstances involved in memorizing something has been shown to increase the likelihood of future recall. So, attaching a funny fact or a location to a name can improve the likelihood of getting it right. If you're desperate, try to think of a celebrity or sports star they resemble and mentally tag them with that label (e.g., "that's Jason, who looks like a young Dwayne "the Rock" Johnson).

I typically have students line up outside the classroom before entering. This accomplishes a few things. First, you can check the state of their uniform (if your school has one) as well as their overall demeanor before they get in the room. Second, lining up outside the classroom helps a lively group settle down before they enter; and third, it allows you an opportunity to strike up conversations using student names and build a rapport in the process. Regardless of how you do it, the moral of the story remains the same—make the learning of students' names a priority.

LESSON 3: TEACH AS IF YOU'RE TELLING A STORY

Teaching in schools is organized around the concept of a "lesson", which involves imparting a few ideas or skills over the course of an hour to a group of what is typically 25 to 30 students. Lessons are then taught sequentially as part of a unit of work, which incorporates a series of ideas or skills within a larger hierarchy of related concepts.

People love stories; it's part of what makes us human. Therefore, I would endeavor to plan your lessons and larger units of work in the same way you would write or tell a story. That is, units of work and lessons should each have a beginning, a middle, and an end. Within a unit, lessons should serve the same purpose as a chapter would in advancing the plot of a book.

Let's consider a situation in which you must plan a six-week unit of work involving what would seem like a fairly prosaic topic— the weather. Done poorly, this topic could be stone-cold boring. However, with a little creative framing, this subject can be quite entertaining. Let's work through an example in the context of a Grade 8 Science class. Please note, although I will discuss an example in science, the principles and strategies underlying unit and lesson planning described in this section should be applicable to any subject you teach.

First, examine the range of concepts or skills that you must teach. Whether planning a unit of work or a single lesson, I would recommend starting with what some teachers call the "hook", which is an idea or activity designed to capture students' attention. In this case, I would craft a Grade 8 Science weather unit around the concept of disasters. By definition, disasters are impactful. You're more likely to have sustained student interest in a topic if you frame it in terms of something that students may have some personal experience with (in the case of weather disasters, think tornadoes, hurricanes, etc.).

Planning a unit of work

When planning a unit of work, start with a top-down view and identify the "big idea" or concept that you want students to learn. In this case, the idea is that the Earth has an atmosphere that creates all of the varied weather we experience. To understand the concept of the atmosphere, students must first have some knowledge about the concept of particles, atoms, molecules, energy, the structure of the Earth, and the position of our planet relative to the Sun. Without a basic understanding of those concepts, it is difficult to make subsequent learning about weather and its causes "sticky"; that is, to make learning memorable and persistent in memory and to embed usable skills. Knowledge can be compared to a spider web, in which individual concepts occupy intersecting points in a larger network of ideas and patterns. For example, a person can't properly comprehend the concept of "a water molecule" if they haven't encountered and understood the linking ideas of atoms and particles.

When I am unsure of where a class is starting from in terms of skills or knowledge, I will have students complete a "word web". This involves giving them a prompt in the form of a central organizing word (such as "weather") and having them attempt to make a spider-web of related words they already know. I typically work through one branch of the word web as an example (such as the "clouds" branch in Figure 1 below) and then have them attempt the rest. Here's an example that shows the approach a student might take:

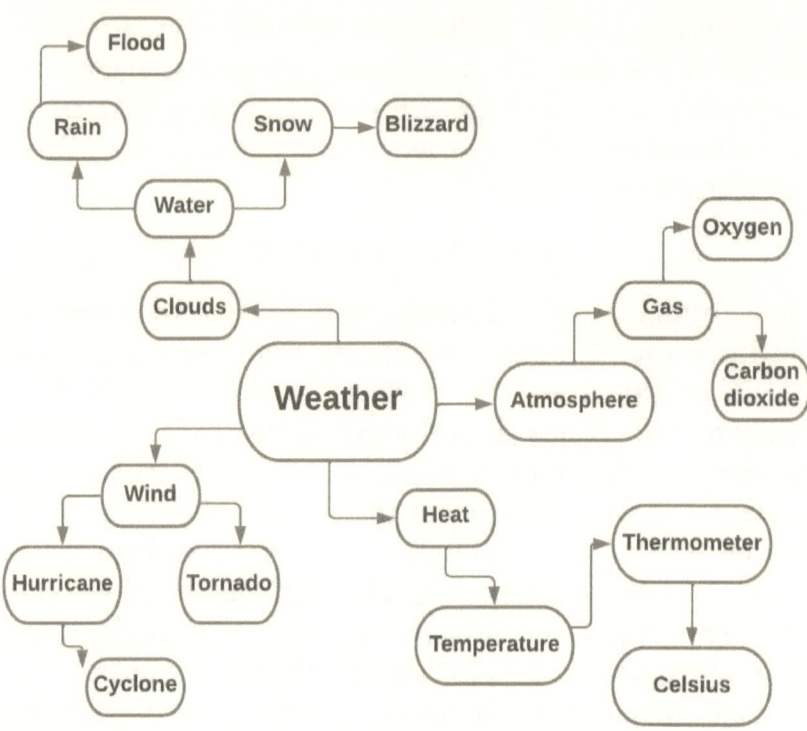

Figure 1: The "word web": An example of a starter activity useful for assessing a student's prior knowledge of a topic. I recommend having students create one using a central organizing word (i.e., the big idea they are learning about) at the beginning of a unit of work. This gives you an opportunity to assess their prior knowledge about a topic.

In this example, some words give rise to multiple branches while others terminate in one or a few words. The purpose of this activity is three-fold: first, it gives you an indication of where the students are starting from in terms of knowledge; second, it can clarify in your mind which topics to introduce or reinforce as preparation for new learning, and third, it is a relatively good proxy for a student's working literacy level.

Let's sketch out a unit of work on "weather" that you might teach to a Grade 8 Science class. In this case, we will organize it around the context of natural disasters.

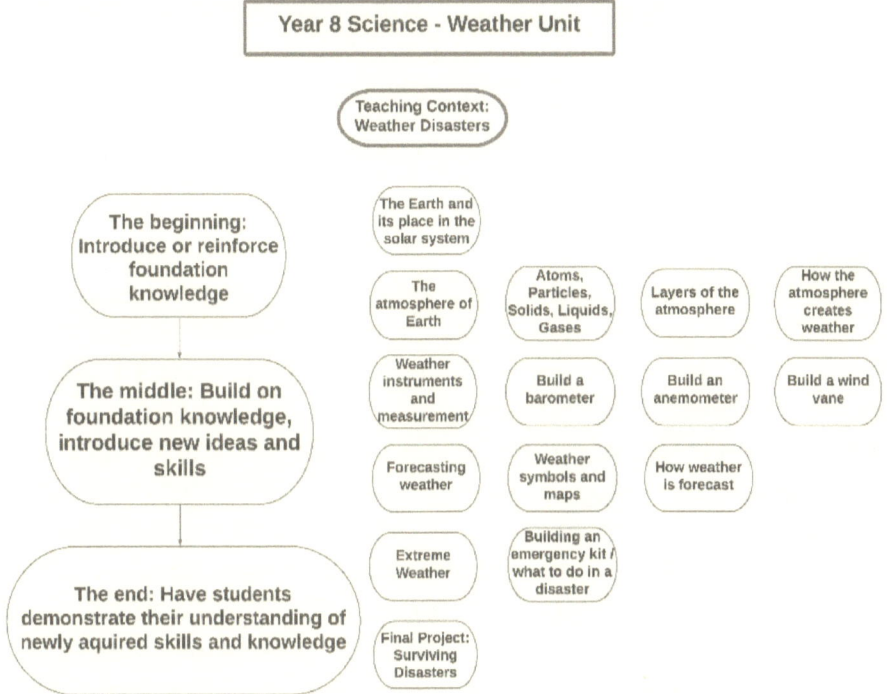

Figure 2: A "big picture" unit plan for teaching weather to a Grade 8 Science class. The large bubbles on the left explain the general learning strategy for the notional beginning, middle, and end sections of the unit. On the right are smaller bubbles, each representing a possible lesson topic to support knowledge/skill development.

As you can see, I have followed a "beginning-middle-end" approach to unit planning. The "beginning" phase involves introducing and reinforcing the essential concepts or skills that are required to understand novel or new ideas. At this stage, an informal assessment of student knowledge or skill level may be required to ascertain the range of starting points you are teaching to. In the middle phase, students are introduced to new ideas and skills in an order that makes it possible for each concept to be "stacked on top of" or "linked" to a previous concept the student is already familiar with. As an example, it makes more sense to introduce the concept of weather instruments and measurement prior to the skill of interpreting a weather map and all of its associated symbols, units, and conventions.

Planning a lesson

In 1977, NASA (the North American Space Agency) launched the unmanned spacecraft Voyager 1. Since that time, it has been speeding away from Earth, exploring the outer regions of our solar system as it recedes into the depths of space. On the 14th of February 1990, NASA used its camera to take an iconic photograph of Earth from some 6 billion kilometers away, capturing an image of our planet that would be the inspiration for Carl Sagan's famous book "Pale Blue Dot: A Vision of the Human Future in Space". Go ahead and search for it on the internet: "Voyager 1: Pale Blue Dot". Although the photograph quite literally consists of a white pixelated smudge on a hazy black background, it is worth having a look at. It is one of those rare photographs that are truly perspective-inducing when you understand the backstory (and as a science teacher, it's quite meaningful to me). As I will describe, I use this photograph as the start of my very first lesson in a Grade 8 Science unit on weather.

Why on Earth would I start a lesson like that? More importantly, what does it have to do with the weather? I begin the very first lesson with the students sitting in the classroom, lights darkened, with the pale blue dot photograph as the first slide of a slideshow projected onto the front board. I start by asking students what they think we are looking at. At this point, not many hands are raised; often, I'll get a few guesses such as "Is it a star?" or something similar. I then skip to the next slide, which shows another photograph ("Cassini: Earth and Saturn - The Day Earth

Smiled"). In this case, Earth is a slightly brighter speck of light visible just beneath the shoulder of Saturn's rings. I repeat the process, this time arriving at a photograph of Earth taken from the moon by astronauts. Finally, I show a photograph of Earth from orbit, with the hazy glow of the Earth's atmosphere hugging the outline of our planet as the blue of the ocean gives way to the blackness of space. At some point during this sequence of photographs, more and more hands go up—we've been looking at Earth all along! In the final photograph, I say something to the effect of *"this is what we're going to explore* (pointing at the atmosphere, clouds, and weather systems)—*Earth's atmosphere and weather, the reason why we are able to survive on Earth but not on other planets."* At this point, approximately five minutes have passed in the lesson.

What I have described in the previous paragraph is "the hook"; a teachable moment meant to engage and frame the context for the lesson's forthcoming learning. The best hooks and lesson starters involve back-and-forth discussions between the teacher and students, in which everyone has an opportunity to demonstrate and explore their prior knowledge and relationship to a topic. Educational theorists regard these activities as forms of "co-construction". As an approach to student-centered learning, co-construction has many benefits; not only will students feel a greater sense of ownership in the learning process, the teacher will also have a better understanding of their students as a consequence (which is a pre-requisite for building good relationships in the classroom).

Following the slideshow, I move to a nearby lab bench, where I have a practical demonstration ready to go. At this point, I ask for a volunteer to come up and assist me in demonstrating an experiment on air pressure (and by extension, the existence of Earth's atmosphere), which might go something like this:

Me: *"So Eddie here has volunteered to help me out in demonstrating what we're going to do next. Eddie, I want you to shuffle this deck of cards."*

(Eddie shuffles the cards)

Me: *"I'm going to draw a card from the deck and I want you to confirm for everyone that this is just a normal playing card."*

(I draw a card randomly from the deck)

Eddie: *"Yep, that's just a normal card."*

Me: *"Okay, so what I've got here is a small glass jar and I'm going to fill it up with some tap water."*

(I fill the jar about half-way)

Me: *"We're then going to put the card on top of the half-filled jar of water and flip it upside down over the sink. What do you think will happen?"*

At this point, Eddie or someone else in the class might offer their thoughts on what might happen to the card and water in the glass jar. I ask other students their opinions and then reiterate the instruction to do the experiment over the sink. Asking a student to help you serves a couple of functions. One, it creates a bit of competition between students as to who will be picked to help with the demonstration; many students want to be the one picked to be up on center stage. Second, asking students to help out with the card shuffling (although strictly unnecessary) creates some dramatic tension, in the process begging the question *"Could Mr. Welsman really be trying to trick us?"*. I usually conclude this with another instruction on the logistics of the practical, such as:

"When I say "Go!", I want you to get into groups of two and have one person find a sink while the other person gets the jar and card. Remember, do the experiment over the sink and mop up any water with this towel if you spill anything. Any questions? Go!"

I like to use *"Go"* as my signal word for transitioning between instructions and student action. Otherwise, you'll end up with students getting up and starting while you're in mid-speech. At younger ages especially, students need clear "start" and "stop" instructions. If students are working and I need to get their attention, I use a "clapping hands" audible signal, usually something rhythmic that requires some deliberate attention to mimic. For instance, I will clap my hands like this:

"Clap, clap, clap-clap-clap" (slow, slow, fast-fast-fast)

If I get a staggered-out, poorly mimicked attempt at the above, I will repeat it again. By that point, everyone is usually listening.

From here, I let the kids go at it. What should be discovered in this experiment is that the card, along with the water in the jar, doesn't fall. Instead, the card appears to "stick" to the jar. After about five minutes, I will get the attention of the students and ask what they have observed. I will then introduce a new variable into the experiment, such as "what happens if you increase the volume of water?". In this particular experiment, there are two factors at play: first, the air pressure in the room is greater than the air pressure in the air above the water in the jar. This means the card is, in a sense, being "pushed up"; second, there is also surface tension and adhesion keeping the card in place under the jar. I use the point about air pressure to expand on the idea that the air around us is in fact made of "something". This serves as a transition to discussing the idea that air is a gas made of moving particles and that the air around us comprises the atmosphere.

By the time I complete the above activity, approximately 35 minutes will have elapsed, leaving you 25 minutes or so in the lesson. Aside from having the students do clean-up, what do you do with the remaining time?

Always have something up your sleeve

As in life, in education you will usually find that you will get half as much done in twice the time you originally thought. However, for those rare moments where the kids have completed all their work and the classroom is tidy, make sure you have something up your sleeve to make use of the remaining time.

One of my favorite end-of-lesson activities is a game called "Survivor". It is a good form of formative assessment/practice assessment, as well as a fun way to get the kids competing to show what they know. Alas, I can't remember where I learned the game, or who invented it. Whoever it was certainly understood how to stoke competitive instincts. First, start by explaining the rules, which go something like this:

"Ok, now we are going to play 'Survivor'. It is called Survivor because the winner is the last person standing. We will start by having everyone stand up with their chair behind them so you can easily sit down and stand up. We will begin by asking a question. The first person with their hand up will have a chance to answer it. Don't raise your hand until I say 'Go!'. If you're chosen and you get the question correct, you get to vote down one person. Be strategic, vote down someone you think knows their stuff! If I say 'wildcard question', the question is open to anyone sitting or standing. The last person standing wins. Any questions?"

You can use this game for revision, to run out the clock on a lesson, etc. Adjusting the number of "wild card" questions you throw in will help maintain class engagement as you near the end of the game and/or adjust the length of the game according to your needs. I have found this to be one of the most reliably engaging activities to finish off a lesson. Sometimes I will start off a unit of work with this game, so as to gauge student understanding of the knowledge required for the unit. You could also use this game to finish a unit by having students create the questions and answers on a piece of paper and having them drop them in a box.

Alternatively, you could use programs such as *Kahoot!* to fill the gap. I use Kahoot quite a bit in the classroom. It is a web-based interactive quiz platform that allows you to facilitate interactive quizzes on a display in the classroom. Participants join using a code and use their devices to tap answers for a range of question types such as multi-choice, true and false, etc. You will find a variety of teacher-created content on a range of topics that you can either use directly or duplicate and edit. Kahoot is great for formative assessment (i.e., a practice assessment that you can use to gauge student progress). Just a tip—when running a game, make sure you go to the settings and toggle on "random nickname generator". This randomly assigns nicknames to the students for display on the scoreboard that gets displayed during the game. Let's just say kids can be quite creative in coming up with inappropriate nicknames if you leave that aspect of the game up to them.

Another useful web-based app for formative and summative (final) assessment is Easy-LMS. This particular program allows you to create courses, assessments, and quizzes. It also collects data on student performance that you can then collate for later use. I especially like the quiz feature. You can also administer a quiz to students via distribution of a URL address; not only do you get the feedback for later analysis; the program creates a "leaderboard" that can be displayed at the front of the classroom to show which student currently holds the highest score. You'd be surprised at how competitive students can be when trying to climb to the top!

Having completed a finishing activity in the form of some sort of game or competition (think Survivor, Kahoot, etc..), the lesson will be complete. Often, I will end a lesson by assigning an "exit question," which any student in a particular table group or row can answer to release the whole group for recess or lunch. The purpose of the exit question is just to briefly recap the lesson and bring things to a close, while also reminding the students of where we started and what we have learned. Overall, a lesson such as the one I have described will have consisted of perhaps three activities. Generally, the younger the students, the more activities and transitions I recommend. For the lesson I have described, we had an "opener/hook" (the astronomy slideshow), the practical (the upside-down jar and playing card trick), and a finisher (the "Survivor" game). Generally, you will find that as students get older, the time for direct instruction (talking to and with the class) can lengthen in proportion to student attention spans. Regardless of student age, I would recommend that lessons follow the "storytelling" format, which includes the following:

i) an "opener" or "hook", to engage student interest in the topic;
ii) a "middle", in which student understanding of the topic is deepened through a group or self-directed activity; and
iii) a "closing/concluding" activity (often done as a group), which serves to tie-up loose ends, assess student understanding, correct misconceptions, and to ensure students understand how their new knowledge sits within the context of the larger topic they are learning about. Having a group discussion or summary at the end can be especially valuable, as it is a practical way of gaining group consensus about what has been learned or accomplished.

In the case of the lesson I have described, the purpose of the lesson was to introduce the concept of the atmosphere and what it is made of. As a final step, one could then give a hint as to what the students will learn about next; i.e., "tomorrow, we will learn about how the atmosphere creates weather".

LESSON 4: DON'T REINVENT THE WHEEL

When starting out as a teacher, you will be busy planning units of work and lessons, selecting and designing activities for your classes, and getting to know your students, your school, and your colleagues. In recent years, there has been a vast increase in the number and diversity of electronic resources available to teachers as a result of both commercial and peer-to-peer publishing. In this section, I will identify some of the marketplaces, websites, and software packages I have used to save time, differentiate my teaching according to student needs, and make the learning process more engaging. In Table 1, you will find a list of the most useful websites and software packages I have used in my teaching.

Table 1: Web-based services and resources for classroom organization, management, and teaching	
https://edublogs.org/	
To create "blogs"	I create blogs for each of my classes with embedded links to other websites, as well as job lists and supplemental work for fast-finishers. This is very useful if you are having students use devices to work through tasks. Essentially,

	you can put your lesson plan on the website and students self-manage their progress.
https://www.teacherspayteachers.com/	
Marketplace for teacher-created resources	Shop for resources created by teachers for teachers. A great source for printable resources.
https://phet.colorado.edu/	
Interactive simulations for mathematics and science teaching	A fantastic and free source of interactive simulations for all things related to mathematics and science.
https://www.teachervision.com/	
Marketplace for educational resources	Offers a subscription service for educational resources created by both teachers as well as educational publishing houses.
https://schooltube.com/	
Video-sharing platform for schools	Hosts videos curated and shared by teachers and schools.
https://www.lucidchart.com/pages/	
A diagramming and flow-chart creator	Useful for diagramming unit and lesson plans
https://www.arduino.cc/education/science-journal	

Turns your phone into a data collection device	Measure and record ambient light, sound intensity, pitch, acceleration, barometric pressure, magnetic fields and compass heading.

LESSON 5: FILL THE POOL BEFORE SWIMMING

As a field of research and professional practice, education is notorious for being subject to the ebb and flow of competing theories. Examples include debates over direct instruction vs. self-guided learning / learning as inquiry, teaching to cater for multiple intelligences, and the relative importance of skills vs. knowledge as focal points in a curriculum. I am not an educational researcher; as a teacher, I see the evidence for or against these learning paradigms in my everyday experience. In my view, these debates are often mis-framed by their proponents; in general, there is some kernel of truth (or at least practical utility) represented by the ideas put forth by both sides of any particular war of ideas. However, one of these debates, on the relative importance of knowledge vs. skills, seems to be a recurring point of contention and conversation in education departments of universities as well as school staff rooms.

Skills vs. Knowledge

Skills vs. knowledge: Which should be emphasized and take precedence in the curriculum? On the surface, the distinction between skills and knowledge would appear to be self-evident; nevertheless, it is worth considering what these words mean in practice. Knowledge refers to information that can be recalled (either in isolation or used together) to assist in making observations, inferences, or conclusions. Skills are rule-based processes in which inputs (consisting either of physical objects and/or mental abstractions) are variously re-shaped, combined, or otherwise manipulated to create an output. As with inputs, outputs may consist of physical objects and/or mental abstractions. The following example illustrates the difference between knowledge and skills in the context of literacy: Knowing that a cat is a "living thing" that comes in different colors (and that white is one such color) are examples of specific knowledge "points". Forming a sentence in which the adjective "white" is used to modify the noun "cat" (e.g., "The cat is white") is a skill that draws upon: a) pre-existing knowledge of the idea of color, b) the specific concept of "white", c) an implicit understanding of what adjectives and nouns are, and d) how an adjective can modify a noun. You can see that writing a simple sentence requires considerable pre-existing knowledge. In many domains of everyday life, knowledge must often precede skill development.

Fill the pool before swimming

One of the most important roles of a teacher is to establish the level of understanding of a student before introducing new ideas or attempting to teach new skills. For some educational theorists and practitioners, memorizing times tables and the learning of facts has fallen out of favor. I think this is a grave mistake. One of the purposes of education (at least up to early high school) is to provide a student with an enduring foundation of knowledge. A store of factual knowledge is useful to have in that it reduces "cognitive load" when attempting to solve novel problems or when employing high-level skill sets. After all, in attempting to solve an advanced physics problem for example, one does not want to be mentally "weighed down" by the demands of figuring out how to rearrange an equation from first principles when the real challenge is to identify the known and unknown variables and to select the appropriate physics equation to solve the problem.

Consider also what "creativity" entails in practice. On the surface, we recognize creativity as a process that results in the production of something new or novel. In reality, many forms of creative expression and/or productivity in the domains of science, engineering, and the arts most often involve incremental advances or subtle rearrangements of existing ideas. The deeper the knowledge "pool" one can draw upon, the more complex and/or original the new product(s) might be. Skills are employed in a similar fashion in the creative process and to perform tasks in everyday life; the analogy of a skill "pool" that one draws upon is equally apt. Because skills are process-oriented, they involve the manipulation of pre-existing cognitive tools or objects; in that sense, they pre-suppose a knowledge base one can draw upon.

Here's the rub—the group of students sitting in front of you will invariably have knowledge "pools" of different depths. As a pre-condition of creativity and of further learning, ensuring that a minimum common knowledge base has been achieved should be the first goal of every teacher. Therefore, when planning units of work or a lesson, particular care should be given to the range of knowledge "points" that are presumed to have been mastered. For example, if one were teaching a Grade 10 student how to read the volume of liquid in a measuring cylinder, it would be important to first verify that they are familiar with the meanings of the unit abbreviations on the side of the cylinder. Understanding the meaning of unit abbreviations represents a knowledge "point" that would likely have been covered in a primary school mathematics class. Many of these knowledge point checks can be done as part of the direct instruction related to the primary learning objective (in this case, reading the volume of a liquid). For example, one could say:

"We have our measuring cylinder here. On the side, you can see there are little lines going all the way up in groups of 10. Here we have mL at the top—what do you think that 'mL' stands for?"

While explaining any task or concept, it is useful to have little "checks" sprinkled throughout the discussion. If you find that the students seem to get these checks right time after time, you can decrease their frequency as the lesson goes on, confident that the required knowledge pool is present.

Appropriate consideration must be given to the comparative importance of skills and knowledge in a student's learning progression. Rote learning of facts is useful to create a foundation upon which further skills and knowledge acquisition can take place. Furthermore, one cannot assume that a knowledge pool of suitable depth exists for all students. Knowledge checks, both formal and informal, may be necessary to gauge student readiness for new learning and skills acquisition.

LESSON 6: RESPECT THE ROOM

It goes without saying that the classroom is where the learning happens. Nevertheless, it is worth discussing the physical environment of the classroom, as it can be an underappreciated and neglected aspect of discussions on student learning. Aside from the obvious basics such as appropriate ventilation, heating, lighting, and seating, the most important concern in maintaining a classroom is creating a space which differentiates it from the other spaces students inhabit throughout the school day. More on this point in a bit.

If you have your own classroom, you will have the luxury of deciding the seating and table configuration that works best for you and the subject(s) you teach. In the first instance, aim and advocate to have your own classroom (though don't be surprised if this isn't possible). Consider a scenario that could happen at a large school, where you might be what is called a "nomadic" teacher. That is, you have no permanent classroom of your own, instead teaching in up to four or five rooms on any given day. In such a situation, it would not be uncommon to encounter situations of environmental contrast. In room A, you might find yourself walking into a clean, well-maintained space, with subject-specific posters and student work hung neatly on the wall. This would be a classroom in which a general atmosphere of care might be evident. Compare that to room B, where you might teach a different class. Arriving in this room, you find rubbish on the floor, chairs scattered about—a picture of general disarray. Now ask yourself, which room would be more conducive to learning? The answer, though self-evident, is worth elaborating on.

I think it is fair to say that in schools, the physical space creates the mental space. Treat your room (and those of your colleagues) with respect. Psychologically, a clean and inviting room tells students what you value and by extension, what you expect. Furthermore, you might be surprised by the chaotic environment some students live in at home. Creating a refuge of order in your classroom can be a singularly instructive oasis of calm for children coming from such environments. If you do have your own classroom, do the cleaning (better yet, have students do it at the end of each lesson), put up some examples of the type of work you expect, and make the space reflect the subject(s) you teach. Doing this will make it more likely that student attitudes and behaviors will mirror those you expect as reflected by the state of your room. And if you find yourself teaching in someone else's room—don't be inconsiderate; clean up your mess. Make cleaning up after an activity or experiment a routine and part of your expectations, which brings us to...

SECTION 2: LIFE IN THE CLASSROOM

LESSON 7: SET SIMPLE EXPECTATIONS

"Be a good human."
"Make good choices."

I didn't come up with these expectations. Rather, I have adopted them from other teachers working in a very effective junior school teaching Grades 7 and 8 boys. I like the simplicity of these expectations. First, they are memorable and short—you want expectations to be talking points that both teachers and students can remember easily. Second, these two specific expectations accommodate a range of situations and can serve as tidy reference points for discussions with students when things go wrong. On your first day of class, make the learning of your expectations a priority. Let's consider the following scenario to illustrate how you might use these expectations when managing student behavior:

Michael is an energetic Year 8 boy who has trouble sitting still. He has been tapping his pen repeatedly on his desk, much to the annoyance of a nearby student called Nathan, who has attention deficit hyperactivity disorder (ADHD), as well as issues involving anger management. Unnoticed by his teacher, Nathan has been growing increasingly frustrated by Michael's vigorous pen tapping. Having reached boiling point, Nathan throws his glue stick at Michael, while also exclaiming "Shut the $%^ up!". Fortunately, the glue stick misses Michael, instead bouncing off the wall next to him.

What do you do?

There are a number of ways one could deal with this. First, you have to respond and deal with the behavior in some way. Doing nothing is not an option. The glue stick in this case could easily become something sharper in the next episode if this behavior were to repeat itself. Second, if you ignore it, you are in a real sense condoning the action, thus setting a tone and the atmosphere for further problems down the track with these students. Plus, it could be that Nathan was on-edge already and that the outburst is a reflection of something more serious going on. Assuming that the pen-tapper (Michael) is unaware of the impact of his habit, I'd recommend dealing with Nathan first. Asking "Could we talk in the hall please Nathan?" would be a good start. Try to do this firmly, assertively, but calmly. Then have a conversation with the student out of view of the class but with your body positioned in the doorway, so you can have a semi-private conversation while still being in full-view of the class. This achieves a couple of things. One, you are not leaving your classroom (only leave your classroom if *absolutely* necessary, as you are responsible for the safety of everyone in the room). Second, you can't be accused of doing or saying anything untoward if your body is still visible to everyone. Third, the student being questioned won't feel as if they are being publicly admonished; this will de-escalate the situation and make it more likely that a frank and truthful conversation can be had.

Once in the hall or otherwise out of view, I would ask Nathan about which of your expectations he didn't meet and have a brief (30 seconds should do) conversation. Make sure the student acknowledges and understands the consequences you are setting. At this point, if your school has a "time-out" system, I would use it and send the student to another supervised location to defuse. If you don't have a system like that and you must have Nathan back in the room, I would recommend having him sit in the hall until you could arrange for him to apologize to Michael (while also informing Michael that he needs to stop the pen-tapping). The send-out/time-out option should be used in any situation where violence, verbal attacks, or repeated low-level defiance occurs.

What if the glue stick had hit Michael? In that case, an escalation of consequences would be warranted (e.g., detention etc. in addition to the send-out/time-out). This should be followed by a phone call or email home on the same day to both parents involved. Where there is any potential for accounts of verbal or physical abuse to be taken out of context or miscommunicated by students to their parents, you want to be proactive in communicating how you as a teacher dealt with the situation. You would be surprised at how often parents will believe their children's account of what happened in preference to yours. It's always better for you to be forthright (and most importantly, *first*) in communicating with home about how you deal with things in the classroom.

In conclusion, I would highly recommend that you make simple, no-nonsense expectations the centerpiece of your approach to managing student behavior. Much trouble and strife can be avoided when you have clear and comprehensible expectations that can serve as reference points in conversations with your students.

LESSON 8: COMMUNICATE PROACTIVELY

This won't be a long section. The golden rule in terms of communicating and working with parents and caregivers is to communicate often and to do so earlier rather than later. Good communication is pre-emptive. One of the best pieces of advice I have ever received came from a parent at a parent-teacher interview:

"I don't mind bad news, as long as I'm warned that it is coming."

With respect to teaching, that means making sure that parents are informed of their child's progress well before a bad outcome is manifest. To fulfill your professional obligations to parents and students, I would recommend sending out regular emails. These might include the following:

   a) A general letter of greeting, introducing yourself, the structure of the course or class for the year, and how/when you can be contacted;
   b) Periodic letters indicating the timing and nature of exams or assessments;
   c) Notices indicating times and locations of opportunities for revision, as well as the various resources available to support students in their learning;
   d) Letters alerting parents to situations where a student is failing to "keep up", accompanied with suggestions as to

how they might catch up.

Here's another piece of good advice that's stuck with me regarding communicating with parents:

"Always make your first contact home a positive experience for the parents."

In practice, this could mean the introductory letter home I just described (even better—try making it a phone call). Psychologically, it is far easier to accept bad news (and trust the messenger of that news) if you at least are familiar with the person delivering it. Another way of building good relationships is simple phone calls home to praise a reluctant student about some recently completed work or a particularly good lesson. I had a colleague at one school who made it a practice to make one phone call a day (about anything, positive or negative) and phone the parents of their entire class at the beginning of each year.

Good communication with parents is especially important for students with challenging behaviors. For parents who are accustomed to bad news when they answer a phone call from the school, you will occupy a particularly good place in their books if you communicate those instances of good behavior or outcomes.

LESSON 9: BE FUTURE-FOCUSED WHEN WRITING REPORT CARDS

Oh, report cards! In theory, the premise is simple; report on student progress, while offering constructive feedback to parents and students. Should be easy, right? Do them well and report cards achieve exactly that purpose. In practice, report cards can be a bit of a minefield. Like writing email, tone is paramount. In this chapter, I will outline a general approach one could take when writing reports and offering feedback on student progress, as well as giving some concrete examples of how one could convey difficult messages tactfully.

What I outline below applies to situations where you are reporting on student progress in a single subject, as you might when writing report comments for students in a secondary school setting. I'm a fan of the "hamburger" approach when it comes to reporting. First, start with a general statement describing the learning context or the topic of work. For instance, with respect to the Earth Science / weather topic I discussed in an earlier chapter, one could say:

> In Science, Mark has been developing his understanding of the causes and consequences of weather.

In the second sentence or two, you could describe his achievement or current working level with respect to the curriculum:

Mark has been developing several Nature of Science skills, including the development of models to investigate how various aspects of weather can be measured. He has demonstrated a comprehensive understanding of the scientific conventions and vocabulary associated with weather events, as well as an ability to accurately measure aspects of weather using instruments he has constructed.

Then, offer some constructive advice (*aka* the bad news, if required) as well as some feed-forward comments on how he might improve his performance with respect to the assessed skills or knowledge:

Mark's attention to detail can be variable. When writing, he could re-read his work aloud to one of his peers to double-check that the intended meaning of his written work is conveyed accurately.

In the chart below, I have drafted several categories of report comments dealing with behavior and attitude, which are often the most difficult to tactfully report on. As you can see in Table 2, it is better to offer suggestions on what you want a student *to do in the future*, rather than commenting on what they have *done wrong in the past*.

Table 2: The fine art of diplomacy, also known as report writing

What you might be thinking...	What you could say instead...
This student talks a lot.	When taking part in class discussions, _____ should make active listening a priority, so he doesn't miss out on instructions.
This student needs	When completing an assignment, _____

to make better use of their time.	should aim to break the project up into smaller, more manageable "chunks", so that he might finish tasks on-time.
This student can be a bit too nice and will let other people in his group "freeload" off of his efforts.	_____ is a diligent worker. As such, when working in a group, he should try not to take on too much responsibility. Instead, he could encourage others to take on a fair share of the work.
This student will sometimes let his peers do all of the work.	When working as part of a team, _____ should articulate what he can contribute and fulfill (to the best of his ability) his obligations to the group.
I want to encourage this student to work independently.	When attempting to solve a novel problem, he might find it helpful to explain the issue to one of his peers. The act of discussing problems to others often has the side-effect of bringing to light new perspectives and potentially new solutions.
This student will only work on things that interest him.	_____ will work proactively on tasks for which he has confidence. When he finds tasks challenging or less engaging, _____ should nevertheless give the task a try so that he can achieve the success that he deserves.
This student has trouble staying on task.	_____ must treat each day as one more necessary small step towards a bigger goal. At times, his attention to the task at hand wanders. This aspect of self-management will become

	increasingly important to his success in future years.
This student's work is sloppy and he doesn't seem to care about the quality of his work.	His attention to detail can be variable…
This student needs to be nicer to his peers.	____ should always keep in mind how he would like to be treated by others and act accordingly when interacting with his peers.
It's okay that your child didn't succeed this time; in fact, failure can be informative.	Though ____ didn't achieve a top mark on this particular project, I have given him some constructive feedback in class that should be helpful in approaching assignments of this type in the future.

LESSON 10: GET ANGRY BEFORE YOU GET ANGRY

One of the best pieces of advice I ever received on managing conflict in the classroom was given to me by a senior colleague early on in my career:

"Get angry before you get angry"

Although adolescents can be incredibly fun to work with, you will doubtless encounter student behaviors that will challenge your patience. In this case, what my colleague was getting at was the idea that you should think about what you do before you do it. First, remember that you are the adult in the room and second, that everyone has bad days. Keeping those points in mind, here are a few tips to prevent your emotions from getting the best of you:

1) If you need to discuss a student's behavior or academic performance with a colleague, do it in the staffroom or close the door (you'd be surprised who might be listening and remember, kids can hear better than you can, even when they pretend otherwise).

2) If you have to use your "angry voice", make sure you do it with a witness around. For instance, if you're having to give someone a reprimand in the hall, keep your body in the doorway and be visible to other students. As we'll discuss later, one false accusation of misbehavior can ruin

your career.

3) This can be a hard rule to follow; but ask yourself: "Would I be comfortable repeating what I am about to say to this student to their parents?" If not, rephrase what you were going to say, walk away, or count to ten.

4) The world is a small place. That student you are referring to could be the nephew of your colleague, or the step-sibling with a different surname of the student overhearing your conversation. Again, if you wouldn't say it to the student's face or to their parents, just don't say it.

5) If a colleague begins to disparage a student or a colleague, make it known that you don't engage in those types of conversation.

6) Walk away from it all at the end of the day. Join a gym. Take your dog for a walk. Just get away from work and try to have a life outside of teaching. It will help.

LESSON 11: DON'T BE TOO NICE

"You're too nice!"

You may end up taking some professional development courses on behavior management as a newly-minted teacher. In those courses, they might tell you that as a teacher you will deal with difficult behaviors, not difficult students. There's certainly no denying that a history of abuse, neglect, and/or poverty may manifest in challenging behaviors in the classroom. When those factors are not at play, the tribulations of adolescence can usually explain most other cases of difficult behavior or low-level tom-foolery. But sometimes, people with great parenting and comfortable lives simply have their personality set to "difficult". Whatever the cause is, you will encounter such individuals at some point. In this section, I will outline some strategies for managing challenging behaviors that may disrupt your class and your mental peace.

Don't be too nice

That was me at the start of my career—too nice (I was told as much too!). If you're considering a career in teaching, it's more than likely that you tick most or all of the boxes for being an agreeable, caring, patient, and socially-minded individual. Couple that with the fact that a teacher's *raison d'etre* is to help people succeed and you have the potential to be more forgiving or accommodating than you should be when bad apples pop up. One of the uncomfortable truths you must accept is that people can't be given personality transplants. Like a photographer bringing a scene into focus, the general dimensions of personality become increasingly fixed as a person nears adulthood. If you're dealing with what appears to be a difficult customer in Grade 9, chances are they will be more or less the same in their senior year; don't try to cure them of their personality. People will often grow out of a difficult personality, but sometimes, they don't.

As Spock famously said, "the needs of the many outweigh the needs of the few". The same philosophy applies with managing difficult behaviors. Don't spend so much time on managing the difficult behavior that you overlook the well-being and learning needs of everyone else in the room. If that means removing students for a timeout, a whole lesson, or petitioning senior management to have the student removed for a longer spell, so be it.

Though no two people are the same, difficult personalities are like ice cream; that is, they usually come in a few common flavors. With that in mind, what follows are some personality profiles of the general categories of challenging personalities you may encounter and my recommended strategies for dealing with them (I have used male pronouns arbitrarily).

The Center of the Universe

So named because they are the center of their own world (and therefore everyone else's). As a consequence, every classroom activity and outcome must be suited to their interests and their desires. This type of person is made more problematic if their parents enable their worst instincts. My recommendation is to keep this type of character active and engaged in everything. If there is a job to do, get them to do it; in doing so, you'll give other students the breathing space they need.

The Enabler (otherwise known as the silent assassin)

Usually of above-average intelligence, this individual is the puppet master who facilitates all sorts of problems ranging from low-level mischief all the way up to the planning, cinematography, and social media distribution of fights (but using other people's phones or fake social media accounts of course). In the causal chain for any problem, their involvement may be buried so deeply that a forensic expert would have difficulty pinning the blame on them. Be prepared to potentially deal with parents who believe in their innocence, so document every piece of evidence you have.

The Ticking Time Bomb

As their name suggests, this student's reaction to adverse circumstances (or even petty annoyance) is often expressed as violence. Usually with a history of fights or bullying on their school record, this person probably has an underdeveloped prefrontal cortex or has been the victim of trauma or abuse in the past. Whatever the reason for their violent tendencies, they need to be monitored closely. This means you don't turn your back on them during lessons, position their desk out of arm's length of other students, remove pointy objects such as scissors from reach (yes, I'm serious), and always count back any tools-that-could-be-weapons (such as dissecting scalpels etc.) following their use in the classroom. I recommend sitting them close to the door, so as to facilitate a quick exit from the room should the need arise. As always, never leave the classroom unattended if you have one of these students in the room.

The Underminer

A close relative of the "Enabler" and so named because they have a talent for undermining the efforts of you or your colleagues, this type of person is socially adept and of above-average intelligence. How you manage your classroom, what you say, how you dress; nothing is beyond the scrutiny of the underminer. Be especially vigilant in managing your professional and pedagogical affairs around this type of student; the underminer's parents are hearing about your shortcomings every day at dinner.

The "Old School" Bully

One of the more common types of difficult personalities you will encounter is the old-school bully. For them, physical and emotional bullying of others is entertainment. Many theories have been proposed as to the motivations underlying bullying. However, the theory I find most compelling is that bullies simply have an unrealistically grand view of themselves (as opposed to compensating for something). Leave the empathy training to the psychologists and guidance counselors. In addition to referring the bully to the aforementioned specialist, the best thing you can do for everyone involved is to make it clear to everyone through your actions that you won't tolerate bullying in your classroom or on duty. So be visible around the school, be alert, and work with other staff to document and report the details of bullying when it happens. Documenting every instance of bullying (and your response to it) gives the senior managers and decision-makers in your school the best chance of putting into action the mechanisms they have in place to deal with it.

LESSON 12: NATURAL JUSTICE IS THE GOAL

Teachers wear many hats. Day to day, teachers may be called upon to serve as the police officer and judge both in and out of the classroom when conflict between students occurs. Conflict may range from low-level disruption in the classroom, up to chronic bullying, theft, drug use, vandalism, and physical assault. How you prevent, react to, and manage these forms of conflict and their repercussions will be an important part of your job as a teacher.

Natural justice

At some point in your teaching career, you may be invited to work as a dean or its equivalent. In New Zealand, a dean is responsible for the academic and emotional well-being of students. To this end, deans monitor student academic progress and mediate any disputes or conflict that might occur both in and out of the classroom. Sometimes, they are called upon to mediate intractable or especially difficult disagreements involving students and teachers. If you get the opportunity to work as a dean or its equivalent, I would highly recommend it as it will help you develop useful conflict resolution skills.

Working as a dean illustrated to me the importance of acknowledging the principle of "natural justice" when investigating and resolving situations of conflict. Natural justice requires that everyone is given a fair and unbiased hearing when assessing evidence and drawing conclusions. This means that everyone is assumed to be innocent until sufficient evidence has been gathered to show otherwise. It also means that you have to keep an open mind in each situation; a student's past history or reputation shouldn't bias your thinking or beliefs.

Teachers and the law

As a teacher, you do not have the same powers of search, seizure, or restraint that a police officer has (your specific powers will vary according to the jurisdiction you teach in). Therefore, you would be well-advised when taking up your first job to ask specific questions about your legal ability to search and seize student property and whether you can physically restrain a student and under what circumstances. As a classroom teacher, you will be called upon to react to (and report on) situations of student conflict that could result in consequences ranging from detention all the way up to expulsion. What follows are examples of how I have responded to typical situations of conflict both in and out of the classroom; be advised that how you *should* respond will vary depending on where you teach, the laws governing your jurisdiction, and the specific policies of your school.

Theft of property

Managing disputes involving theft of personal property has taken on significant importance in recent years. More often than not, instances of theft involve personal electronic equipment such as earbuds/headphones, mobile phones, and laptops. Mobile phones in particular have become preferred targets of theft, given their importance in social communication and their monetary value (it's not uncommon for mobile phones to cost thousands of dollars). Many schools have resorted to the installation of cameras, which has significant benefits with regard to narrowing a list of suspects and corroborating alibis. After all, cameras don't lie. However, many instances of theft won't be caught on camera, as they will often occur in "hidden" locations such as bathrooms or changing rooms. In any case, when something goes missing, you may be called upon to assume the role of the investigator.

Take good notes

Knowing your students and their social networks can help in determining motive and the trustworthiness of their accounts/reports. Taking note of details such as where the item was last used/seen and communicating the theft to other teachers across the school can help in the event that a similar item is seen being used by a student in another class. When gathering evidence, writing down detail is key. It is especially important that the person being interviewed sees you writing down what they say; in my experience, the act of having your words transcribed can prove stressful to guilty parties and prompt an inadvertent admission or revealing contradiction in what they say. Your school will likely have a student information management system into which incidents of misbehavior or conflict can be documented. At least in my country (New Zealand), what you report on in a student information database constitutes a legal record. Therefore, it is imperative that what you report and write is factually accurate and suitable for reading to other parties such as the student's parents/caregivers, as well as law enforcement and child protection agencies. Another point: privacy laws often require that you not identify other students by name when making an entry into official school records for a given student. In such cases, using the other students' school identification number may be more suitable than using their name. For example:

"Martin reported that his phone went missing during the first period Tuesday 25 March. He reported having seen student 4523 going through his bag earlier in the period."

When you have no leads

Let's consider a specific example of theft in the classroom. A student informs you that an item has been stolen from their bag. Sometimes, this will be a prank by friends and the item will be returned by the end of the class. When you have no clear leads on who is responsible, one of my preferred techniques is the amnesty return system. When the item has been reported stolen, I'll stop the class and make an announcement:

"It seems a _____ has gone missing from _____'s bag. Here's the deal: if it's returned to the school office as a lost and found item by the end of the day, that will be the end of it. Otherwise, _____ will have to get involved."

As for the last blank, fill that in with whomever is tasked with sorting out serious misbehavior in school. Senior managers responsible for pastoral or student welfare are generally selected for their ability to navigate complex social problems. Students also see their involvement as a sign you are taking things seriously.

The strategy described above has worked for me in the past; if it's a prank, the item is usually returned by the end of class. If it's not, it allows the culprit an opportunity to return it anonymously. The trick here is that you have to live by what you say; if the item is returned as per the amnesty opportunity, you have to abide by it. The objective is to get the item back; if the adult in the office happens to observe who dropped it off, take note of that for future reference. Although your innate sense of right or wrong is usually inclined to pile on further punishment to the culprit if you find him; remember, you have to live by your words. If you strike a bargain with the class, follow through on it. With the amnesty opportunity system, you should also communicate to the victim's parents or caregivers the approach that you are taking (and do this on the same day). From a parent's perspective, getting the item back is usually the priority, while laying down punishment on the guilty party is usually a secondary concern.

Let's assume the item doesn't get returned via the amnesty system. In the intervening time and depending on the value of the item that was stolen, you will hopefully have had an opportunity to do your background research on the likely culprits and to do some individual interviews. The principle of natural justice should prevail: only take action on the basis of good evidence. By this point, you should also have called in senior management to assist you in investigating the theft. Unfortunately, sometimes it is not possible to recover stolen items.

Prevention is the best cure

To prevent theft, never leave your classroom unlocked or leave your students unattended with other students' bags or belongings. When taking students to locations such as the gym or the library, have students leave everything but the items they need in a locked room. Finally, it often is helpful to set down a "bring at your own risk" policy; many schools explicitly state in their enrollment forms or contracts that they won't be held responsible for the loss of personal property such as expensive mobile phones or computers. That can be helpful in limiting your liability. Finally, if your school allows you to confiscate items such as mobile phones etc. when they are being misused, be aware that you are doing so at your own risk. Make sure your school has a system for securely storing such items until they can be retrieved by a parent or caregiver.

The school-yard fight

Social media has changed the nature of violence in schools. It used to be that the consequences of fights would rarely spill over into the outside community—social media has changed that. Nowadays, videos of a fight can be distributed widely and quickly via a variety of social media apps. Social media is often used to instigate, plan, and/or promote conflict well in advance of the actual event. In the next section, we will discuss scenarios in which you happen upon a fight, as well as what you might do afterwards.

Responding to violence

A fight may break out in the classroom or the playground. When it does, you have a couple of options based on your proximity and how progressed the fight is. Remember that what you do and what you say is probably being filmed and is likely to be distributed over social media. As mentioned previously, you should follow the specific advice given by your school or employer regarding any response to instances of violence in or out of the classroom. What follows are my opinions on the general issues that must be considered when responding to incidents of physical violence and how the aftermath of assaults has typically been dealt with in the schools I am familiar with.

Following a fight, the first priority is to see to the safety and well-being of everyone involved. That could involve referring the students to the school nurse or sick bay for checking (especially if concussions are suspected) as well as separating the students involved. Students should be accompanied to separate locations in the school office where they can be interviewed and the situation diffused. In New Zealand, you cannot forcibly confine a student (this is known as seclusion); if a student is to be isolated from other students in a separate room or place, they must have a clear means of exiting the room unimpeded and must also believe that they can leave the room or space freely. If they leave the room despite instructions not to, then you cannot compel them to stay. Make sure that you ask your senior manager or Principal what the law is in your country regarding isolation of students.

Obviously, separating students following a fight provides the necessary space and time for everyone to calm down. Ensuring students are in a safe location also serves the purpose of keeping everyone involved safe from interfering friends and/or family (this includes adult family members). Remember, just because someone is an adult doesn't mean they can be trusted to respond rationally to situations of violence involving their child. Make sure that parents or caregivers are informed promptly about the fight; you do not want parents or caregivers to hear about it second-hand via other channels. Following an assault, it is often requested that parents either pick up their child directly from school, or if that's not possible, to verify that the student has a safe way to get home following dismissal. What you don't want to happen is for the people involved (or their friends) to start up the fight again later in the day or after school is dismissed.

Sometimes, physical assault is one-sided; that is, there might be an imbalance of size and strength between the combatants, or the assault might be one-sided in terms of intent. These are the instances where it is important to be vigilant to prevent assaults before they happen. That means ensuring that your classroom is not left unattended and that your school's playground supervision system is adequately staffed etc.

Physical restraint in situations of conflict

In New Zealand, the Ministry of Education permits teachers to use physical restraint only as a last resort and to prevent "imminent harm" to themselves or another person. Such situations might include breaking up a fight, preventing a student from using a weapon, running onto a road, or throwing furniture. Keep in mind that the laws on physical restraint and the use of force vary by country; make sure you ask your principal or manager what the law is for your locality. Your school should have a handbook or set of policies that outline how you should respond to specific situations of conflict and violence. If such a document does not exist or specific examples on how to resolve conflict are not otherwise articulated, you could ask the following questions to clarify your responsibilities:

1) Under what circumstances can a teacher restrain a student? What does restraint involve? What kind of records do I need to keep if an incident involving restraint occurs?
2) What procedures should I follow if I come across a fight or find out that one has occurred?
3) Who is responsible for communicating with parents or

caregivers that a fight has occurred?
4) What are the procedures for resolving the consequences of a fight?
5) If a student cannot be in class or take part in regular school activities as a result of conflict in or out of the classroom, where are they to be and how are they to be supervised?
6) What types of conflict are expected to be resolved by the teacher? How do I record these incidents and my response to them? Who should I go to for help if I can't resolve an issue?

Resolution of conflict

In recent years, there has been increased attention paid to the restoration of relationships as part of the conflict resolution process. Known as "restorative justice", this method of conflict resolution places an emphasis on the restoration of relationships and having the wrong-doer identify and acknowledge the harm done to the victim. Proponents of this method of conflict resolution argue that in acknowledging the harm done to the victim, the guilty party is more likely to empathize with the victim and is therefore less likely to repeat the crime again. To illustrate how this principle might be applied to a typical situation of conflict in a school, consider an example involving theft. After determining who the guilty party is, a series of conversations would occur in which the perpetrator would be guided to draw conclusions about why they acted in the way they did and to acknowledge the harm done to the other party. In the case of theft, they would have to acknowledge that in stealing something from someone, they are depriving the victim of something that may have been costly in time or money to obtain. By undergoing guided conversations with the perpetrator, it is thought that the victim also gains some sense of closure over the incident. People who favor this method argue that it is more effective as a method of preventing recalcitrance than traditional punishment and that it assists in repairing relationships between the perpetrator and the aggrieved party.

Criticisms of approaches to restorative justice

Critics argue that it is unlikely to be effective in situations involving people who cannot "empathize with the victim" (whether that is a consequence of personality or their age). Another line of criticism centers on the importance of consequences as signals for defining boundaries within complex social settings (as schools no doubt are). They argue that though restorative conversations may help repair relationships, such conversations cannot provide "signaling" value to communities in terms of what is right or wrong.

In my experience, the most effective forms of conflict resolution at the classroom and school-wide level draw on a variety of methodologies. These include strategies drawn from traditional approaches, in which a particular transgression results in a predetermined consequence (i.e., if you do x, then y will happen etc.), combined with elements taken from the restorative justice approach. For instance, in an example of student conflict involving theft, a good outcome should involve the following:

a) The aggrieved party has their property restored
b) The perpetrator must bear the cost of righting the wrong (i.e., they must replace the property of the victim if they can, or otherwise compensate the victim)
c) The perpetrator must acknowledge what they did and apologize to the victim
d) A "visible" consequence occurs along with the restorative approaches described above

For example, depending on the severity of the crime, the guilty party might be assigned a detention, be suspended/stood down, or in extreme or repeated cases, be excluded from the school (i.e., expelled). This would serve as a "signal" or "deterrent" to other members of the school community. This reasoning has merit because other students would generally not be privy to the restorative discussions conducted between the wrongdoer and the victim. Consequences such as detention, suspension, and exclusion can act as "stop signs" or "boundaries" to provide tangible signals of what is and is not acceptable behavior within a school community.

In education, there is also a community of thought in the conflict resolution field that whenever possible, consequences for misdemeanors and infractions should be logically congruent with the crime. For instance, a teacher who found that a particular student was routinely late could "add up" the missed minutes of class and assign a detention to make up for the missed work time. In this sense, missed time is "paid" with time. Though this consequence follows logically, unfortunately it often requires that the teacher "pays" with their lunch or break time as well. For this reason, many schools run centralized detention systems supervised by a dean for this purpose.

In my experience, it is desirable to have logical consequences for misdemeanors whenever possible, if only because it allows you to easily justify the consequences you assign. In summary, the most effective conflict resolution systems at both the classroom and school-wide level accomplish the following:

- a) They right the wrong for the victim,
- b) They have signaling value to deter repetition or imitation of the act, either by the perpetrators or other members of the school community,
- c) They provide opportunities for the wrong-doer to advance their understanding of why the action is undesirable and/or harmful for themselves or others, and
- d) The consequences repair the relationship between the wrong-doer and the victim

Whatever the consequences and methods of conflict resolution that you apply, they must be fair and proportionate, which is the

JOHN A WELSMAN

subject of the next lesson I learned as a beginning teacher.

LESSON 13: KIDS ARE FAIRNESS DETECTORS

As a teacher, your day-to-day work will tend to make you a bit of an amateur psychologist. After all, you will spend a significant amount of time poking around inside people's heads, attempting to figure out what motivates them. One of the principles of classroom management that you will soon discover is that above all else, kids care about fairness. So, what does this mean in practice and how do you employ it in a typical situation where the entire class seems to be uncooperative and unmotivated? Consider the following (albeit extreme) scenario:

It's your last lesson on a Friday afternoon and you have your Grade 10 class. It's the end of a pretty intense week and you're feeling exhausted. You've let the class into the room and they just won't come to attention as they normally do. Everyone seems to be talking and your entreaties to listen up and stop talking are going unheeded. What do you do?

You've got a few problems here. First, you can't narrow down the culpability to one or a few students; more or less the whole class is talking. Second, you're at the end of your tether and don't have much energy for intensive behavior management that involves working the "whole" room. Let's deal with these issues separately.

First, remember that students are natural "fairness detectors". If your classroom management techniques are arbitrary and unfair, you're going to be pushing a rock uphill in your attempts at classroom management. In this case, picking a random individual here and there to reprimand for their inattention not only does not make sense, it would be patently unfair. After all, it seems like a whole-class problem. In this case, I'd recommend that you turn around, breathe deeply, and think of one simple task or job that you could write on the board as a "starter". It could be something like:

> *Do now: Form a group of four and elect a speaker, a reader, a writer, and a noise monitor.*

Then, walk over to the row or group of students closest to the door and quietly ask:

> *Ok, we're going to try this again. The whole class is going to leave everything here and line up outside the door.*

It's important that you do this in a conversational tone, directing the instruction to a few students at a time as you walk through the room. In situations such as these, instructions are more likely to be followed by an individual or a few people in close proximity to you, as opposed to you broadcasting the message in exasperation at the whole class.

When you have the class outside the room and they're waiting in the hall, wait calmly and quietly. Eventually, they *will* get bored of standing there. Those who get bored first will typically bring their neighbors to attention and make a point of admonishing anyone nearby who is still talking or carrying on. I would recommend this approach for situations such as this because you have to employ a method which treats everyone the same way, rather than arbitrarily picking and punishing. As I said at the beginning, kids are fairness detectors. Once you have their attention, simply state the instructions you have written on the board, adding that you will explain the rest once they're in the room. At this point, if you feel you have restored a sense of calm, let the students back into the classroom. If the new instructions and process of lining up don't result in a change of attitude, repeat the process again for the whole class. Ninety-nine percent of the time, this strategy will calm everyone down the first time and allow you to get on with the teaching.

In this scenario, the starter task involving the group of four is intended to facilitate easier classroom management for you and to make students more individually accountable. The first benefit is that students are put in a position in which they must self-delegate and self-manage. Often, your most challenging students will respond well to being appointed to a place of importance in a group or having a defined "job". Secondly, it encourages accountability and fairness (and you'd be surprised at how willing kids are to enforce accountability on each other). After all, if you're the noise monitor for your group and you haven't told your group to quiet down; well, that's kind of on you, isn't it? Having students appoint themselves/each other to different roles within a group allows them an opportunity to self-differentiate according to their strengths. For example, if you can't write well, chances are you can speak to your ideas or instead be the noise-monitor for your group.

After checking that each group has the required roles filled, give your next instruction. This should be the "meat" of the lesson. Perhaps you want students to read two pages out of a novel and then craft a paragraph in response to a related question you write on the board. Whatever it is, outline the instruction and emphasize the role each person in the group will serve. If you don't have full command of the room at this point and you can tell that attention spans are wandering—don't try to teach from the front! Instead, have the simple instructions on the board and simply rotate from group to group, repeating instructions, monitoring progress etc. *It's easier to command and sustain attention from a group of four rather than a group of thirty!* And if in talking to a particular group you are ignored or your efforts dismissed—well, that's defiance and it's at that point that it is *fair* and *justified* for you to send individual students out of the room for the rest of the class (and any effective school will have a "time-out" system in place). If there isn't a time-out system, raise the issue as a matter of priority. Sometimes, the only solution is to remove students from the room.

LESSON 14: YOUR VOICE IS YOUR MOST VALUABLE TOOL

At some point in your teaching career, you will lose your voice. Whether it be due to a nagging cold or chronic overuse, you will discover at some point that without your ability to project and control your voice, sustaining student attention and controlling a room becomes much more difficult. A teacher's ability to modulate the tone, pitch, and volume of their voice is therefore an indispensable skill that you must develop if you are to preserve your voice and be successful in the classroom.

The way you sound to other people is a lot different from the way you hear your own voice, due to the differences in air pressure inside and outside of your skull and the configuration of your inner ear. Therefore, before you step into a classroom, I would recommend recording your own voice. Note that this recording will represent your voice under the best of circumstances; that is, in the absence of stress, fatigue, or competing noise. Do this first for something scripted that you read off a page. Now repeat the process for something unscripted; pretend that you are explaining a task or answering a question. Better yet, do this experiment in an empty classroom and by imagining that you are talking to a person in the far corner of the room while you make your recording. Doing this will give you a better sense of how you actually sound to other people. If you don't mind subjecting a friend or your partner to the recording, play it for them. Whether it is to yourself or someone you play the recording to, ask the following questions:

1) Were any parts of the recording difficult to understand?
2) Do I speak too fast or too slowly?
3) Do I use pause-fillers such as "um" or "uh" when speaking?

How you sound when you're under stress

When you're under stress, your vocal cords constrict and tighten. In stressful classroom situations, such as when you're caught off-guard or just plain getting angry, this may result in the pitch of your voice increasing (and your voice may "crack"). If you don't make an effort to counteract this, you will put your voice under considerable strain and in the worst case, find your voice "cracking" or losing it altogether. What follows are some strategies for controlling and preserving your voice.

Start loud and end with a whisper

This one is quite useful. It takes some practice but works remarkably well. When giving an instruction to the whole class, start "loud" and then make a deliberate effort as you are speaking to lower the volume of your voice with each successive word. What you will find is that students will quiet down as you speak as they strain to hear you, creating a feedback loop in which you can reduce the classroom noise level while preserving your own voice.

Wait for full student attention before giving instructions

This is another strategy that takes some effort. After all, if you're short on time or patience, your natural tendency will be to want to talk over students. Avoid this whenever possible. Whatever your system for gaining attention is (whether a 3,2,1 countdown, of the rhythmic clap we discussed earlier), use it. Giving instructions while trying to gain students' attention will only stress you and your voice.

Try to speak from the belly

Controlling the pitch, tone, and volume of your voice is challenging. Your voice is at its best when you're relaxed and speaking with someone in close proximity. As soon as those conditions change (as they certainly will in the classroom), things become a bit more challenging. Before you step into a classroom for the first time, do a bit of practice training your voice.

When trying to project your voice across a room, first make sure you're getting enough oxygen; so, breathe! Second, do some practice in an empty room. When practicing, try putting one hand flat under your belly button. As you speak, imagine you are pulling the sound out of that region of your body. What you are aiming for is to keep the pitch of your voice "low" even as you project your voice with increasing volume. Again, it takes a bit of practice, but you will become better at it over time. It's important that you try to minimize the amount of "loud" talking that you do. After all, you could be in a classroom for upwards of five or more hours a day and you don't want to be operating your vocal cords at full throttle all of the time. So, to preserve your voice, use other classroom management strategies to minimize the competing noise that might otherwise require you to speak more loudly than you want to.

Use a student helper

The following is a technique I use with classes that have especially short attention spans, or when you feel like you're playing whack-a-mole with respect to interruptions (for example, when you have just got the attention of one side of the room and the students in the back corner start talking again):

Me: I need a volunteer who has a watch or a phone with a timer (someone then puts up their hand). Thanks Jimmy. I'm going to demonstrate how you're going to do our next activity and it's going to take me 2 minutes to explain. Jimmy is going to start the clock when

I start talking and if anyone interrupts me, he's going to re-start the clock and I'll begin again. Ready Jimmy?

This may sound like a weird thing to do, but it turns attention into a bit of a game (see the next chapter for how "gamification" can make behavior management easier). With respect to the student volunteer, try to pick someone in the class who is respected by their peers (i.e., someone who has influence). When someone interrupts you, the volunteer will stop the clock, you'll have to begin again, and if you've chosen the right volunteer time-keeper, they may do some of the management for you (i.e., *"really, that was like 5 seconds!"*). What also tends to happen is that the people who do want to listen and get on with whatever activity you are doing will end up applying some peer pressure to the people interrupting.

Work the whole room

One of the behavior management strategies that I learned early on was the benefit of "working the room". That is, use your physical presence to help preempt problems, control the class, and thereby avoid having to raise your voice in the first place. The most effective teachers I have observed are always on their feet working the room. Whether it be during a session where students are working independently, in groups, or when giving direct instruction to the whole class, effective teachers will move around and among students in a non-intrusive manner throughout the lesson. If you have the attention of the class and you know a particular student's attention is wandering, casually moving in their general vicinity while continuing to speak will generally preempt trouble or distraction.

Interact with each student at least once per lesson

Another benefit of deliberately working the whole room is that you get an opportunity to inspect student work and the general state of the room as you go. This is especially important in situations involving the use of science labs (think spills on floors etc.) where it is important to be circulating constantly. I had a colleague whose rule-of-thumb was to have at least one interaction with each student in his class during each lesson. The goal of this approach was to keep tabs on everyone and their learning as well as to build relationships. Deliberately walking the entire room during a lesson will go a long way in helping you to achieve this goal.

Eavesdrop (with permission) while a colleague teaches a lesson

Another thing I would recommend doing periodically during your first few years on the job is to observe other teachers teaching as well as "listening" to them teach. Schools will often have a teacher who has the responsibility for inducting/mentoring new teachers. These people are appointed on the basis of their recognized skills in classroom management and teaching pedagogy. Therefore, I would start by observing them. Observations typically involve sitting in the back of the room, watching as a class goes about their business. I would recommend going one step further; try sitting outside of a classroom as a lesson is going on. Not only does being out of sight give you some insight into how a lesson is proceeding (as the presence of an observer can change the classroom dynamic somewhat), doing so also gives you some insight into the teacher's use of their voice as a tool. Pay attention to the frequency with which they interact with the class as a group, how they gain student's attention, the length of time they spend talking to a class at a stretch, and so on. Similarly, have your colleagues observe your teaching and ask them to take note of the same things (or any other issue of concern). Remember, your colleagues are your single most important resource in improving your teaching practice.

JOHN A WELSMAN

LESSON 15: "GAMIFY" EVERYTHING

I remember a particularly astute comment made by one of my colleagues after I shared with him my difficulties in motivating a junior Science class. Without skipping a beat, he said:

> *"It's just a game. Many students will do their best not to learn; your job is to trick them into learning."*

One of the long-standing tropes used in Hollywood depictions of public education is that of the charismatic teacher walking between neatly ordered rows of desks, pontificating on the subtleties of Shakespeare while students listen in rapt attention. Though there may be moments in some classes where this type of lecturing with sustained student attention is both possible and practical, this style of direct instruction is generally not characteristic of how most classrooms actually look or sound today.

We live in the era of algorithmically-induced limited attention spans. Walk any school or college campus and observe what students are doing during their idle moments and you will find that the vast majority are glued to some app on their smartphone screen. For example, consider the popular app that features short videos tailored to your interests and delivered to your phone on a never-ending virtual conveyor belt. The genius of social media apps in general is that the content delivered to your phone is based on your previous interactions with the app, creating the ultimate self-reinforcing dopamine delivery system. In other words, over time you get more of what you like, over and over and over again. At the level of the brain, each time you see or hear something you like your brain squirts out a little bit of dopamine. Cute puppy in a basket: dopamine squirt; your favorite pop star dancing to a looped fragment of a music track: dopamine squirt (and so on). These apps are notionally "free", though instead of paying for them with physical currency, the user instead gives the app (and the advertisers paying to ply their wares on it) their attention.

It is not my intention to vilify smartphones or smartphone apps. They are a feature of modern life and are useful in a multitude of ways. However, as a teacher, it is important to recognize two important facts:

1) You (and the content/skills you wish to impart) are competing for a limited "span" of neurological attention; and

2) The learning activities you design cannot compete with the dopamine-delivery systems represented by the apps and games that are freely and readily available to students on their phones.

What can you do?

Though banning phones in the classroom could be an immediate solution, it doesn't address the fact that the lessons you design have to "mesh" with student expectations for activities that recruit and maintain their interest in the same way their phones do. Education is a motivation game, so if you want to recruit attention and motivate students to learn, in short—gamify everything that you can. Games are dopamine-delivery systems and serve a useful purpose in psychosocial development. It's no coincidence that the appetite for playing games is especially pronounced among children and adolescents. During these early stages of life, people learn how to work together and compete with one another by playing games of all sorts, either formally or informally. The inclination and appetite for play is deeply ingrained and is a common feature of biological development in the animal kingdom. You don't need to prompt young animals to play; they just do it. Think of the cat playing with a ball of yarn; later in life, that kinesthetic practice that helped to hone its fine motor control can later be applied to hunting birds etc.

Furthermore, the release of dopamine that accompanies play and winning games makes them pleasurable and encourages further practice. Given that the human instinct to play games is a feature of our development and not a bug, why not exploit this appetite by applying the underlying principles of play and games to learning?

Games involve some combination of skill, knowledge, and chance. Many are also progressive (i.e., they have levels). In a real sense, you could say that games reflect the natural learning process, in which competence (i.e., winning) is the product of the demonstration of skills or knowledge iterated over multiple rounds of increasing difficulty. What I suggest is that you should apply the foundational principles of games to not only the activities you plan for a lesson, but to also apply them in how you run your classroom and relate to your students.

Competition is fun

We have already discussed some of the formal games you could run in the classroom (see Lesson 3: Teach as if you're telling a story). In addition to these, you can introduce elements of competition to situations as mundane as taking up a worksheet (yes, I use them and they do have a useful place in teaching). For example, consider what I call "Bill Nye" day. In that same Grade 8 Science class I described earlier, I often run a video quiz once a week when I have that class at the very end of the school day. The rationale: it's the last period, the kids are typically tired out from the rest of the day, and so am I (plus, Bill Nye is great). Though the Bill Nye show was produced back in the 1990's, you would be surprised at how well many of the episodes of the "Bill Nye the Science Guy" show have aged. Incidentally, it's worth watching the Bill Nye show as an instructional exercise in what effective science communication to children looks like.

When we play an episode of the Bill Nye show related to weather, we accompany it with a ten to fifteen question fill-in-the-blank worksheet (you can buy these at a great online marketplace for resources: www.teacherspayteachers.com). The questions follow the order of the video and require students to listen to keywords relating to the theme of the day (think wind, atmosphere, the water cycle etc.). To make this a competition, you could set the scene like this:

Me: Okay, today we're learning about the atmosphere. I would say that if you get 10 out of the 15 questions on the video quiz sheet correct you've done your job. If you get 15 out of 15, you're working at a Grade 9 level.

At this point, you have set up the "goal lines" (i.e., a score to beat). Taking up the worksheet at the end can also be made into a game by having students who answer one of the questions nominate another person with their hand up to do the next question. As an adult, you might think this seems rather uninspiring, but I routinely have Grade 8 classes where the students are practically levitating off their seats, begging to be chosen to answer while the "chooser" dramatically surveys the room to give another student the power of selection. I kid you not, this works really well in junior classes.

The principle of games and competition can also be applied to mundane tasks such as cleaning up the room or monitoring classroom noise levels. For instance, which instruction is more likely to be followed?

Version A: *Nobody is leaving this room until it's cleaned up.*

Version B: *Alright, we've got five minutes left. Who is going to be the first table with all the paper picked up off the floor, chairs tucked in, and standing ready to be dismissed?*

You guessed it; version B works every time. First, version B specifies exactly what will happen and what you want students to do. More crucially, it does so by making it a competition. To paraphrase the comedian John Cleese—you can be serious without being solemn.

Many schools also incorporate competition into their across-the-school behavior management systems. Positive behaviors are rewarded with the student's name being added to a ballot box by teachers across the school. At the end of the week, an assembly takes place where a few names are drawn for a prize of some sort. Being nascent statisticians, students quickly tune into the idea that increasing the frequency of good behaviors results in a greater likelihood of having their names drawn from the box. In the schools I have worked at where this system is in place, it seems to work. I acknowledge that some people will argue that good works should be their own reward; however, I believe such arguments fail to recognize that at the end of the day, everyone responds to incentives, be they of the "carrot" or "stick" variety (plus, our whole economy runs on the premise!).

LESSON 16: BUILD RELATIONSHIPS OUTSIDE THE CLASSROOM

You will not be effective as a teacher if you cannot build productive and positive relationships with students. Obviously, this process begins in the classroom; nevertheless, one of the most effective ways of building good relationships is through extracurricular activities. Typically, this takes the form of structured sports or other cultural activities in which the teacher acts as a coach or mentor.

One of the best relationship-building experiences I have had was the opportunity to work in a boarding house supervising students at a boys' school in the evenings. My responsibilities included mealtime and dormitory supervision as well as running a tutor time during which students would do their schoolwork. In the course of these duties, I would strike up conversations with students in the halls and adjudicate any issues that arose with students living in the dormitory. As a consequence of such interactions, I would get to know how students think, what their home life was like, and how they were getting on in their classes. I've also done the more typical extracurriculars such as academic clubs and sports.

Regardless of what type of extracurricular you choose to involve yourself in, doing an after-school activity of any variety gives you some deep insights into who your students are and how they think. Similarly, your students will have the opportunity to get to know you as a person outside the normal confines of the classroom and to do so in a structured, goal-oriented environment. Extracurriculars are such an important facet of school life that your involvement is usually an implicit requirement of your employment. You will also learn a host of skills such as the planning, fundraising, and supervision of students on multi-day sporting events. As part of your first teaching job, I would recommend finding a sport you are interested in or have experience with and attempt to position yourself as the "second" coach or supervisor. In this way, you "learn the ropes" without having to have full responsibility for a team or club from the very outset.

LESSON 17: OPTIMISM HAS NO PLACE IN PLANNING FIELD TRIPS

Field trips and overnight camps are memorable features of school life. Despite their obvious value for students, they can nevertheless be a source of considerable stress for you if you enter into them unprepared as the supervising teacher. Every school should have a comprehensive set of guidelines and procedures for preparing and running camps and overnight trips. However, if you are tasked with preparing and implementing a new or unique event or trip and no paperwork exists, you have a number of things to consider. If there is one rule to follow when planning field trips, it's this: it pays to be a pessimist.

Plan events and trips down to the hour

When planning a field trip, ensure that you have considered what students will be doing *down to the hour.* As the old expression goes, "idle hands are the devil's workshop". This is especially true when you are considering the management of large groups of adolescents. In my experience, where there have been behavior management issues on a trip, they occur in circumstances when students have had too much time on their hands.

The other reason to consider scheduling events at the hourly level is that it forces you to consider all the health and safety risks associated with any and all activities. Answering questions such as "what are students doing?", "where are they?", and "who is supervising them?" forces you to consider variables such as staffing and scheduling of breaks for supervising adults.

What are your non-negotiables?

At some point in your career, you will encounter a situation in which a student will do something on a day or overnight trip that requires them to be sent home. The expectations in the classroom should naturally carry over into the out-of-school environment; nevertheless, there are additional variables inherent to field trips that may create unique situations requiring special consequences. In my view, there are three categories of misbehavior that would necessitate having a student taken off the trip and sent home. These include a) reckless endangerment of other people or property, b) drug or alcohol use, and c) violence. Reckless endangerment is a catch-all category for any situation in which a student creates or causes a situation where harm can be caused to people or property. Think arson, misusing camp equipment, vandalism etc. Whatever your non-negotiables are, you should communicate these to the students, caregivers, and your school management in advance of the trip. That way, there is no need to justify your decision-making process after the fact. If it has been determined that a student has crossed one of these lines, you must have arrangements in place for someone to meet you and retrieve the student. If that is not possible, there must be a procedure in place for managing the student while remaining with you on the trip, as well as agreed-upon consequences to follow upon their return to school.

Be a pessimist

The political commentator George F. Will once said: "The nice part about being a pessimist is that you are constantly being proven right or pleasantly surprised." Truer words have never been spoken with respect to event management and school trips. In the spirit of that sentiment, you could consider the following questions when planning a field trip and planning for contingencies:

1) If you are using specialized equipment, how could someone misuse it? (Be creative in your thinking, because I can assure you that teenagers are...)
2) If students are in a remote location, how readily could one student get separated and lost from the group? What would you do if that happened?
3) Will students be interacting with members of the public?
4) How will students be supervised or monitored during times when there are no structured activities planned?
5) Will students have access to their phones or devices during the trip?
6) What ratio of supervising adults to students must be arranged? Do you have back-up supervisors for last-minute illnesses?
7) Do any of your students have medical conditions (or behavioral tendencies) that will have to be managed? If so, how?
8) Are toileting, showering, and sleeping arrangements suitable for all students?
9) Have volunteers been vetted (e.g., police-checked) in accordance with school policy or the laws in your jurisdiction?
10) Have your travel arrangements been made with appropriate consideration given to the possibility of disease or disaster-management? For instance, do students need vaccinations or medication if going to a high-risk area? What events (either natural or otherwise) could interrupt the trip? Do you have a contingency plan for such circumstances?
11) Will students be required to carry money? If access to

money will be required, will they carry it, or will you dispense it as required?
12) What procedures do you have in place for managing illness or injury? Are there any first-aid qualified adults on the trip?

"Prevention is the best cure"

Desiderius Erasmus is credited with that insight. Although the phrase "prevention is the best cure" is traditionally applied to health care management and medicine, it is nevertheless a good philosophy to keep in mind with regard to the management of events and school trips. In this section, we will consider some common scenarios you might encounter on field trips and how you could prevent them from happening (and deal with the consequences if they do occur).

The missing student

Priority #1 of field trips is to bring back the same number of bodies you had when you left (and in the same condition as they were when they departed). It's not uncommon to hear stories about students going missing while on field trips. One of the common situations where this may occur is during transport. Consider the loading of 50 students on and off a bus at a rest stop. I would recommend having a stack of printed lists of student names on hand. As they board the bus, check their name off. Before boarding, remind students if they have remembered to bring on everything they left with, such as phones, wallets, hats etc. Once on the bus and checked off, they stay on the bus. I'm not a fan of counting bodies once they have boarded; people can be miscounted and/or missed quite easily in a crowded environment such as a bus. Similarly, when in environments such as museums or other public places, you should specify boundaries which students are not to go beyond, as well as meeting points and times, and a location to go to if something unexpected happens.

Another common scenario in which students may go missing is the hike or nature walk. In such a situation, it's advisable to make rules for the students such as i) no walking in front of the lead adult or supervisor at the head of the group, ii) no-one is to stray behind the adult or supervisor in the back, and iii) if you encounter a fork in the trail or a situation in which you cannot continue confidently, sit down and wait for someone from behind. At periodic intervals, stop and do a count of your students.

Put a twenty in your shoe

I've never gone this far, but one teacher I knew of had students put a piece of paper with a phone number, a location, and a twenty-dollar bill under the insole of their shoes if on a field trip in an urban environment far removed from the student's everyday experience (think of an overseas field trip to a foreign city). The idea here is that if the student were to be separated from the group, they could at least hand a police officer or bus driver the location where they should be, along with a contact number and some money to get there if required. After all, wallets can get lost or left behind, but chances are the student won't forget or lose their shoes.

The moral of the story is to be prepared. Moreover, talk to your senior managers well in advance of the trip about procedures and policies and ask lots of questions. There should be a formal process and set of paperwork for the type and duration of trip you intend to take the students on. If there isn't, ask your senior managers to work through (and sign off on) the plans that you make. You are going out on a limb taking students off-site. In exceptional circumstances, you may even take students out-of-country, which is an especially high-risk scenario. Ask questions, plan for the worst, and hopefully, you will create a memorable and enjoyable experience for the students.

LESSON 18: EVERYONE IN THE SCHOOL CONTRIBUTES TO SUCCESS

Building productive working relationships with your colleagues will be a critical variable affecting your success as a teacher. In a school, no one teaches in isolation; education is probably one of the most collegial of professions as a consequence. Even after you move schools, maintaining a network of contacts in the profession can be very helpful in a range of ways. In this section, we will talk about the ways you can build and preserve good relationships within the education sector.

Know your school's policies and procedures

When starting a new job, ask if there is a handbook outlining school policies and procedures; read these carefully, because they can help you quickly get up to speed on the day-to-day processes that help a school run smoothly. Situations of conflict or disagreements with other staff often arise from misunderstandings involving school policies and procedures. For example, if your school's policy is that you should have field trips booked in on the school calendar a month in advance, knowing and following that procedure prevents you from accidentally double-booking students who were supposed to be involved in some other event (which could disrupt another teacher's plans for that day).

Find a mentor

When you arrive at a new school, find out who is responsible for the induction and mentoring of new staff. If such a person doesn't exist, the most appropriate alternative is likely to be your line manager or supervisor (such as the head of your faculty or department). It also doesn't hurt to approach someone in your school who both students and staff respect and ask them if you can sit in on a few of their classes to observe how they run their classroom. As mentioned in Lesson 15 ("Preserve your voice"), a useful observation practice is to listen in on a lesson by sitting outside the classroom to figure out what vocal techniques and language choices an effective teacher uses when interacting with students and managing their classroom. Moreover, building a relationship with a respected teacher in your school means you have someone with whom you can trade ideas and discuss problems with.

Help can come from anywhere

The administrative and auxiliary staff of a school are the unsung heroes of education. Here I'm talking about the secretaries, teacher aides, janitors / caretakers, school nurses, and canteen staff etc. who ensure the students are assisted, fed, cared for, and given a clean environment to learn in each and every day. They do important jobs; so, try to help them out whenever possible. You'd be surprised at the many big and small ways that administrative and auxiliary staff can help you in return; even a small "thank you" can go a long way in showing your appreciation!

Time is the currency in education

In business, they say "time is money". In education, contact time with students is the currency that matters. With the increasing emphasis on high-stakes testing and assessment, teachers often find themselves counting the hours they have with their students in an attempt to fit in every hour of teaching they can. When I have heard other teachers complain about their colleagues, it's often because a teacher has had to frequently pull students out of other classes to be on field trips, courses, sports events etc.; as a result, they end up missing class time that must then be caught up. Therefore, tread lightly on other teachers' contact time with their students! If you have to take students out of school on a trip or event, try to schedule these things well before exam periods etc. Moreover, communicate your intentions (and preferably offer some alternative times/choices) to the teachers who are affected by your plans.

Watch what you say about your colleagues

Never, never, never disparage another teacher! If there is a golden rule for building good working relationships in a school, it is this: **only say things about a colleague that you would be willing to say to their face!** Nothing destroys productive working relationships in schools like animosity brought about by gossiping, casual disparagement, or off-hand comments about other teachers or staff. In addition to being unproductive, such comments can be self-destructive; who is going to trust a person who casually disparages another person or their work?

LESSON 19: RECOGNIZE THE RIGHTFUL LIMITS OF YOUR INFLUENCE

Teachers often underestimate the influence they have on their students and society at large. If you doubt me on this point, just look to history for an example. During the Cambodian genocide of 1975-1979, the Khmer Rouge attempted to create an agrarian society by means of lethal social engineering. Millions died from famine, forced labor, and executions. Among the victims were teachers, doctors, lawyers, and members of the clergy. Anyone considered intellectual or socially influential was a focus of the regime's murderous efforts. The Khmer Rouge understood that adults in positions of authority could influence the way children (and by extension, adults) think and make decisions. Make no mistake—if your students respect you, you will have considerable influence in shaping the way they view the world.

Teachers and their influence

Being a teacher entails responsibility in terms of influence. How you behave, communicate, manage conflict, and interact with students and other staff is noticed by students. Though the children's caregivers are the main source of influence shaping how they think, friends and teachers will also be hugely influential in shaping the way students see and engage with the wider world.

Education should challenge one's mindset. By that, I mean that an education should shake-up preconceived notions, biases, and errors of thinking. We are born with a set of instincts and cognitive biases that can easily give rise to false beliefs if left unchecked and unchallenged. This is especially true with respect to the way we view the world. For example, it was entirely reasonable for people living in previous eras to believe that the Earth was flat, or that the Earth was the center of the cosmos. It's not hard to see why such beliefs became established. The observation that the sun sets and rises is congruent with the mistaken belief that the Earth must be fixed in space and the sun revolves around it. Only by careful observation of the Earth's movement relative to other celestial bodies was it established that the reverse was true. Erroneous beliefs can arise from a number of sources, either through the application of what one might call "common sense" or by cultural inheritance. Much of a teacher's work is devoted to correcting false beliefs or the habits of thinking that give rise to them, either by providing new ways of looking at things or by teaching cognitive skills that protect against errors of reasoning.

Having one's beliefs challenged can be destabilizing. Childhood and adolescence are times of significant intellectual change, in which new ideas and perspectives are encountered, experimented with, and often adopted. When changes in worldview occur or long-cherished beliefs are dispensed with, the impetus for change can come from a variety of sources, including friends, school, the media, or by exposure to new cultures.

If you teach in a special character school in which a particular religion is an organizing feature of school life and culture, then the worldview you will teach will very likely be defined in detail. A public school will present a different situation entirely. In such a school, students from all walks of life and religious traditions may be sitting in your classroom. In this context, the stage is set for competing ideas to clash. During the course of your career, you may be asked about your beliefs. This could happen during lessons which touch on any aspect of life for which a religious tradition might inform someone's views or actions. As a Science teacher, I am routinely asked questions regarding my views on religion and politics. So, what are you to do when such questions arise and what is the role of the teacher in such circumstances?

Stick to the curriculum

Teachers are the managers of classroom discussion and debate. These roles must be exercised with self-restraint, as you can easily color students' thinking by virtue of your choice of words and tone. Before we get into specifics, it is worth pointing out that where you teach will influence how you manage student questions. In New Zealand, teachers are trusted to exercise their individual judgment when it comes to the moderation of classroom discussions that arise from the teaching of the curriculum. Note that this is not the case in all parts of the world. Indeed, in some parts of the United States, politicians are actively legislating how (or whether) certain topics are to be discussed in the classroom (as is the case in 2022 in Florida with Republican-proposed legislation on the teaching of critical race theory). Therefore, if you find yourself in a place where the teaching of contentious topics is the subject of political action, it is worth asking your school management if there are any state or local school board/district directives dictating what you can and cannot discuss in the classroom. Personally, I am an advocate for a high-trust model in teaching and the exercise of individual teacher judgment when it comes to the moderation of classroom discussions (incidentally, I would argue that New Zealand is a rewarding place to be a teacher because of the relatively high level of trust that the government and parents have in teachers).

The intellectual autonomy of the student

The classroom should not be a teacher's personal soapbox or pulpit. Leave the politicking to the politicians and the sermonizing to the ministers, priests, rabbis, and imams. In a secular school, the role of a teacher with respect to the introduction and appraisal of ideas should be to help students build a cognitive toolkit that can be applied to the situations and problems they encounter in life. In New Zealand, the cognitive toolkit that teachers are expected to develop in students consists of five key competencies: thinking, using language, symbols, and texts, managing self, relating to others, and participating and contributing.

When teachers present their own beliefs as "fact" they run the risk of violating a student's intellectual autonomy. Children have a right to learn without being indoctrinated. Teachers can inadvertently sway opinion simply by holding and espousing certain beliefs. One of the questions I am routinely asked in the context of discussing evolution or astronomy is "Do you believe in God?". My strategy with such questions is to tactfully skirt the issue by steering the conversation back to the science curriculum with comments such as "Science can inform our knowledge of Earth's history and how living things evolve but at present, it doesn't allow us to say anything conclusive about what happened before the Big Bang or why." If pressed on the issue, I will say something like "It's not my job to teach you about religion." Such answers are generally unsatisfying to students but nevertheless provide an important signal to them; namely, you will not tell them what to think. Students (and parents) will respect you for this. Instead of offering your opinion, emphasize that your job is to give them the skills to think for themselves. This is especially important in situations where students subscribe to views that run contrary to all the available evidence. Viewpoints and ideas based on false premises or faulty logic are unlikely to be overthrown as a result of dismissive or sarcastic comments made by a teacher. A better strategy is to help students build an effective cognitive toolkit and to introduce them to different viewpoints. This is especially important in the age of social media and search engine optimization, in which software and mobile apps tend to direct you to *more* of what you have sought out or signaled approval of (or interest in) in the past. An important job of the teacher is to introduce students to alternative ways of viewing an issue that is normally excluded through such filters. Overthrowing bad ideas and misinformation is not an instantaneous process. It is important to remember that bad ideas tend to burn away over time if you apply sufficient friction to them in the form of well-supported evidence and reasoned arguments.

LESSON 20: DEVELOP MICRO-HABITS TO GO THE DISTANCE

It's 2022 as I write this. The last few years have been a period of constant upheaval in education, as students and teachers adjust to what seems like the never-ending "new normal" of the pandemic. The toll of the pandemic and the accompanying upheaval in workplace and educational practices has been significant. Students in many parts of the world have had to do without the usual features of school life that many of us considered a normal part of growing up. School proms/balls, sports, assemblies, and field trips have been curtailed or eliminated entirely during Covid outbreaks. Combine that with protracted periods of remote learning, having to wear masks while at school, and isolate at home when sick and it is no wonder that student psychological distress has skyrocketed and academic achievement has plummeted in many parts of the world.

My home in the far south of New Zealand (Invercargill) had been fortunate enough to have been spared the initial tribulations brought about by the original Covid strain and the delta variant. However, when omicron arrived in local schools, it steamrolled inexorably through the teacher workforce. The already stretched pool of relievers/substitute teachers was soon exhausted, leaving schools to fill teacher absences internally. This required many teachers to teach above their normal allotment of hours in the classroom, covering for their colleagues who were at home isolating with Covid or caring for family members. Both students and teachers were exhausted. Somehow, most schools in New Zealand remained open throughout much of the omicron wave, in no small part as a consequence of high vaccination rates and the creative restructuring of school timetables as the omicron wave pushed through. In many ways, the pandemic has forced teachers, managers, and education policymakers to reconsider the state of the profession, the way teachers teach, and how students learn. Personally, it has underscored to me the importance of setting boundaries and reasonable self-expectations, something that teachers too often neglect as they sacrifice the necessary aspects of self-care required to "go the distance" and remain productive and healthy over the long-term.

I'm 42 years old as I write this. One of the most important lessons I have learned in my 12 years of teaching thus far is the fact that I am not indefatigable. During my first job, I would routinely stay at work until 8 or 9 PM in the flawed belief that if I devoted ever-increasing hours to lesson planning, student engagement and achievement would advance in equal proportion to the hours I put in. Looking back, I realize that was a flawed view. To be effective and responsive in the classroom, a teacher must be alert and focused. Being "switched on" requires that you are well-rested, which presumes that you have had sufficient opportunity away from work for rest and relaxation. Given the varied and many competing demands on a teacher's time, it is imperative that you use your preparation time outside of the classroom effectively so that you can leave work at a reasonable hour. Over the years, I have developed a number of micro-habits that have been effective in reducing the hours I must devote to lesson planning and resource preparation. These will be the subject of this section.

Aim for one superb lesson each day

Teachers regularly undergo periodic observations of their teaching practice in order to receive constructive feedback and improve their skills in the classroom. While in my first year of teaching, I was being observed periodically by the deputy principal of the school, who had been tasked with mentoring early career teachers on staff. In those early days, I was going full-tilt, probably unsustainably so. During the debrief following an observation of one of my science classes, she remarked "You're going to burn yourself out at the pace you are going!". In this instance, she was referring to the intensity of instruction, interaction, and planning evident in the lesson she had just observed. Expanding on that point, she emphasized the importance of pacing oneself to avoid burning out. Her advice: aim for one superb lesson each day. I have since found this to be particularly good advice for several reasons. First, it sets a self-imposed limit to one's efforts—set a bar, aim to meet it, and be satisfied having met that standard of planning, delivery and classroom management for the day.

In your beginning years as a teacher, you can easily spend the same number of hours as you do in the classroom on unit preparation, resource development, and lesson planning. In light of this, her advice was for beginning teachers to set a high expectation of performance for one class each day. In that class, the aim is to have everything on-point, which should include: a) engaging activities, differentiated according to the various learning needs of your students and b) effective behavior and learning management, in which each student is challenged to deliver on a clearly articulated and personalized learning objective for that lesson. Achieving these two aims for everyone in your class becomes easier over time and with experience; however, in your early years, it will be a stretch to achieve these aims for each and every lesson of the day. By setting a self-defined objective of one superb lesson each day, you accomplish two goals: first, you minimize the "mission creep" that characteries teaching. By this, I mean the tendency for work to follow you home and invade an increasingly larger share of your waking hours as you aim for perfection in every lesson. Secondly, it helps you to be accountable with respect to the management of your own well-being. One of the bad habits that teachers can fall into is over-planning at the expense of personal and family time. Also, try to vary/randomize the "superb" lesson across all of your classes, so that each group of students receives equal attention in this regard.

The one great lesson per day rule is meant to evolve with you. Over time, as you expand your catalogue of resources and lesson/unit plans, you can set the bar higher, so that eventually you are striving for excellence in every lesson.

The 5-15-45 habit

I'm not certain who told me about the 5-15-45 habit and I'm not certain if it was their invention or was borrowed from someone else. A cursory search of google revealed no clues either. In any case, this is a time-management habit that works. Before we delve into what it entails, it is worth looking at a teacher's typical day and how it is structured in order to understand the challenges of time management that teachers face.

A teacher's typical day will consist of varying combinations of time spent in the classroom, on recess duty, in meetings, and doing extracurriculars before, during, or after the end of the school day. A teacher generally does not have protracted periods of time available for lesson/resource preparation, marking, and reflection during the school day. This is in contrast to many jobs involving administrative and/or project-based work, in which a person may be free to decide the structure of their day and how they will schedule and complete their various responsibilities. For illustration, this is how a teacher's day at my current school might look like if that person had a full allotment of classes and no management responsibilities:

8:30 – Staff briefing
8:45 – Period (lesson) 1
9:50 – Tutor time (15 minutes for reading school notices and checking in with a specified group of students once a day)

10:10 – Period 2
11:10-11:30 – Recess / interval
11:30 – Period 3
12:35 – Period 4
1:35-2:20 – Lunch
2:20 – Period 5
3:10 – End of day

Typically, a full-time teacher in a secondary school in New Zealand will teach four periods out of five (and have one day a week with five lessons). Depending on staffing, the size of the school, and the extent of playground supervision required, the equivalent of three recess sessions may be spent supervising students during the school day or before or after school (e.g., monitoring buses or doing road patrol). Generally, resource preparation, marking, and meetings with other teachers will be done outside of the class times shown above. Other activities, such as bathroom breaks and meals, must be taken as and when time permits according to the schedule above. Obviously, teaching does not follow the 9-5 schedule of other jobs, as following this model would leave only one hour and forty-five minutes a day for marking, resource preparation, meetings etc. As a consequence, teachers generally will work outside of these hours. To maximize the efficiency of the time you do have, I would suggest trying out the 5-15-45 strategy.

I have a paper journal that I keep in my office. Each morning before class begins, I write down a list of the tasks I want to complete and assign them a number: either 5, 15, or 45. Each number represents the time I estimate the job will take. Marking will generally take 45+ minutes, so if that needs to be done it is assigned the "45" designation. If I need to write an email to a parent, that might get the "5" designation. Photocopying a set of booklets for a test might get a "15". As the day proceeds, I pick off the tasks according to the time available. What isn't completed one day is carried over to the next and so on. I have found that if my short-term goals aren't structured according to the time available, tasks tend not to be completed in the optimal order. Time is the limiting factor every teacher wishes they had more of. In light of this, I have found the 5-15-45 strategy to be quite effective in managing my time and my achievement objectives.

Keep a record of your efforts

In Lesson 3, I discussed the idea of viewing a lesson as an episodic "story" that might consist of three to four segments or activities. Each of these activities might have some sort of accompanying resource. If you teach secondary school, you might accumulate a significant number of worksheets, unit plans, lesson plans, booklets, videos, website addresses, assessments, and other miscellaneous documents in the course of teaching upwards of five subjects for 20+ lessons per week and 40+ weeks per year. If these aren't catalogued and organized in some accessible and easily modified way, you will end up devoting a disproportionate amount of your time each week to organizing your upcoming lessons. One of the most useful habits I have developed is digital cataloguing of lesson plans.

In addition to cataloguing your resources in an easily accessible manner, it is also important to define and record the learning objectives and success criteria for each lesson *in advance* of each lesson. There is a school of thought in educational theory that argues that learning should "be visible". Implementing the making-learning-visible approach involves a variety of strategies and tools. One of the most important considerations in making learning visible involves the articulation of learning intentions and success criteria to ensure students understand what they are learning and what they should aim to achieve. Having to formulate learning intentions and success criteria for a lesson also requires that the teacher has considered aspects of the teaching process such as student needs, constraints of time, equipment and materials for learning, and the placement of the lesson within the large scheme/unit of learning. As a consequence, having these prepared in advance of a lesson is especially important given the relative complexity of the variables involved. For example, for the unit of work on weather science that we considered in an earlier chapter, the learning intention and success criteria for the lesson might look like this:

Learning intention: *Today, we will build a device that can measure wind speed.*
Success criteria: *I have built an anemometer and measured the wind speed produced by a desk fan.*

In the department of the school I work at, teachers are encouraged to write a "call to action", a learning intention, and the success criteria on the whiteboard for each lesson so as to make the learning for a given lesson "visible":

Do now:
Today, we will…
I have been successful if…

I record these prompts, learning intentions, and success criteria as part of the record of my lesson planning. Over time, I have developed a database of lessons that can be swapped between courses or shared with colleagues, complete with the accompanying resource files and web addresses for any activities required for a given lesson. Up to this point, I have used Microsoft OneNote for this purpose. Each notebook in OneNote is devoted to a particular class. Below is an example of what this could look like for a typical lesson plan:

Unit:	Lesson Topic:	Date:
Do now:		
Today, we will:		
I have been successful if:		
Resource files and		

weblinks	
Extras if required	

I would recommend that you use a software package that allows you to embed files such as pdf's, presentation files, word documents, web links etc. into the lesson plan file itself. That way, you can simply pull up the file and click on the link rather than searching your computer's folders or doing google searches on the spot. A benefit of using a program such as OneNote to catalog your lesson plans is that you can re-arrange them as you re-teach a unit of work or a class over successive years.

At the end of the day, how you decide to record and catalog your lesson planning and resource preparation efforts is less important than the act of doing so. Do not underestimate the amount of effort you will devote to lesson planning and resource preparation over the course of a year. Having invested the time to do so, ensure you have a system to efficiently catalog and store the products of your efforts.

SECTION 3: MANAGING AND OPTIMIZING YOUR CAREER

LESSON 21: PAY YOUR BILLS ON TIME

That was the advice given to a group of staff sitting in a morning meeting at one of the smaller rural schools I worked at. That might seem like an odd thing to say to your employees, but in this case, the principal who said this was getting at a larger point. Your conduct outside of school has ramifications for how well you can do your job in the classroom. If you find yourself working in a small town, people will quickly get to know you. The electrician you call on the weekend for an emergency job might be the brother of a colleague or the parent of a student. How you treat people in the community therefore can affect your student's and colleague's perceptions of you. Teaching is a motivational game that is dependent on convincing people to work with you in a cooperative fashion. Students aren't likely to listen to you if their parents are questioning your character around the dinner table (e.g., "so-and-so never pays his bills on time!"). Though it should go without saying, the point here is that you must conduct your personal affairs with the same standard of professionalism that you would if you were "on the clock" at school. For better or for worse, you are being judged as a representative of the school community wherever you go.

LESSON 22: TROUBLE IS OFTEN THE CONSEQUENCE OF SEEMINGLY SMALL DECISIONS

Although I can't recall his exact words after all these years, this was the essence of a comment made by the principal of a large and well-respected school I worked at. Like most careers, your success as a teacher and your prospects for advancement in the profession will be highly dependent on your reputation. A good reputation is difficult to earn and easy to tarnish, so be mindful of the decisions you make (both big and small) that could jeopardize it.

In education, teacher misbehavior is usually given the label "professional misconduct". There are many examples of misconduct that can unintentionally arise from saying or doing things outside of the workplace which then have follow-on consequences for a teacher's ability to work with their students or colleagues. What follows is a list of some common situations, habits, and mistakes that can put your reputation and career as a teacher at risk.

Table 3: Common situations, habits, and mistakes that can jeopardize your career as a teacher

The situation	What could happen	What I would recommend
Making a phone call to a parent or student using your personal phone.	Your personal phone number ends up in the "public" domain. You end up receiving unsolicited phone calls or texts from parents or students.	Preferably, use a school phone. If you must use your own device, conceal your personal phone number when making calls.
Emailing a parent or a student using a personal email account.	Any disputes or accusations of misconduct can't easily be mediated by school management because communication occurred via a private account.	Use your school email for all communications involving school business. The contents of these emails can then be easily verified by school management.
Being alone in a room with a student.	You put yourself at risk professionally whenever you are in a situation where you are alone in a closed space with another student.	Keep the door open at all times. If the conversation involves the potential for conflict or requires a closed door, hold such conversations in the presence of another colleague.
Transporting students in your private vehicle.	Having a student in your private vehicle is potentially bad "optics" if someone sees you driving alone with a student.	Avoid whenever possible. If it must be done, call a senior manager beforehand (think the deputy principal or above) regarding the reason and obtain permission from the parent/caregiver.
A student lives on your street and asks if they can come by your house to ask a question about their assignment.	You place yourself at risk of accusations of misconduct by the student and outside observers if you entertain students at your private residence.	Never do this. School business and teaching should always be conducted on-site.
You carry out personal business or entertainment on a device provided	Using your device for personal business could unexpectedly reveal your browsing history	Use your own device for personal business or entertainment. Everything done on a school-provided

by your school.	during lessons. Think of the auto-fill function on your internet browser as you google something in front of the class.	device or via your school's internet is visible to your IT department.
You're at a restaurant during a field trip with your class and parent volunteers. A parent offers to buy you a drink.	During school hours and on field trips, you are *"in loco parentis"*, meaning you are legally responsible for student safety and well-being. Alcohol could compromise your judgment.	Don't accept the drink and remind the parent of their responsibilities. Most schools have a clause in their field trip documents stating that staff and volunteers will abstain from alcohol, drugs, and sexual activity while acting in a supervisory capacity on a school trip.
You hold a social event (involving alcohol) at your house. Your colleagues and the parents of some of your students are invited. Unexpectedly, one of the parents bring their son to the party.	Depending on the nature of the event, you (and other staff members and students) may end up hearing about the party the next day, as seen through the eyes of the student who attended.	Recommendation: Avoid such situations by making it clear beforehand that this is an adults-only event. In small towns, this situation may happen. Think carefully about the distinction between school, your private life, and how social events could be perceived by the school community.

LESSON 23: BE DELIBERATE ABOUT WHERE YOU WORK AND WHAT YOU TEACH

Having worked in a number of schools, three facts have become apparent to me with regard to managing a career in teaching:

1) That having a successful career is highly dependent on finding your "niche/fit" within the education sector;

2) That what you teach has a profound influence on your employability and your prospects for advancement; and

3) That each school is unique; being effective in one school does not guarantee success in another setting.

I would propose that these points are broadly applicable whether you are teaching in New Zealand, Australia, the U.S.A, or any country sharing an educational tradition originating in the British tradition. The reason for this stems from the broad similarities in curriculum and school structure in these countries. To illustrate this, I will explain how I came to teach in New Zealand as an immigrant from Canada and how the school system in New Zealand is configured.

Training as a teacher in New Zealand

Training as a teacher equips you with one of the most portable skillsets you can leverage if you are considering moving locally or migrating to another country. I have worked as a teacher for over a decade in public (i.e., government-funded) schools in Aotearoa New Zealand, a beautiful country of about five million people in the South Pacific (and famous for being the filming location of the "Lord of the Rings").

Although I went to college (what New Zealanders call "uni") in Canada, it wasn't until 2009 that I emigrated to New Zealand (this was just after the financial crisis of 2008 that left the economies of much of the world reeling). I had several reasons for choosing New Zealand as a location from which to start my career in teaching. First, when talking to a Canadian teacher during the planning stages, I was told that i) *"if you can teach in New Zealand, you can teach anywhere"* (in reference to the quality of the training and experience you might gain) and ii) *"that a lot of new ideas in education come from there"*.

Before leaving Canada, I was accepted to a teacher training program (the Graduate Diploma in Teaching and Learning) at the University of Canterbury, located in Christchurch, the most populous city on the Southern Island of New Zealand. It was a one-year program designed for graduates already holding an undergraduate degree; successful completion of the program allows you to register and work as a trained teacher. To this day, the job market for teachers in New Zealand remains strong.

The New Zealand School System

The education system in New Zealand has been influenced strongly by the English tradition, though in recent decades there has thankfully been an increasing emphasis on recognizing and embedding the language and culture of the Maori people in the formulation of educational policy, practice, and school culture.

Schools vary widely in size and structure, ranging from one-room schools in remote areas to sprawling special-character urban campuses (i.e., single gender and/or religious schools). In New Zealand, boards of trustees are elected from local communities and manage internal school affairs, structures, and curriculum priorities while operating within the overall framework provided by a national curriculum. The effect of this localized system of school management is to create incredible diversity in school character across New Zealand.

Schools are run by a principal, who is appointed by an elected board of trustees and given broad responsibility over school management in matters ranging from the financial to the pedagogical. Deputy or assistant principals are typically appointed to more closely manage pastoral (student welfare) management and curriculum delivery, as well as day-to-day staffing and school logistics. In schools of larger size, faculties such as Science, English, Technology, etc. are managed by Heads of Faculties, who themselves preside over curriculum and staff management within those departments.

In New Zealand, experienced teachers with graduate degrees can earn up to $90,000 New Zealand dollars (NZD) as of 2022. Management units (of $5000) are added to the salaries of teachers with specific curriculum or special project responsibilities. For example, one additional unit ($5,000) might be assigned to curriculum leaders in small schools or to a teacher in charge of a sports program. At the other extreme, deputy principals in large schools might be assigned upwards of 10 or more additional units ($50,000+) on top of salary in recognition of their extensive portfolio of responsibilities. Principals are paid on a different scale from classroom teachers; the pay range for secondary principals in New Zealand currently ranges from $98,031 up to $171,260 NZD, based on the number of students enrolled at the school.

The school year in NZ runs from late January to early December, with three two-week school breaks every 10-11 weeks throughout the year. Centrally-administered assessments in the form of exams are administered each year beginning in November to students in Years (Grades) 11 to 13. Those "senior" students earn credits in those exams and throughout the year in other teacher-assessed tasks to qualify for NCEA (National Certificate of Educational Achievement) qualifications, which range from Level 1 (Year 11) and up to Level 10 (PhD-level attainment). I won't dwell further on the nature of New Zealand school assessment; the focus of this section is to help you choose a teaching subject and school should you find yourself looking for a job.

Choosing your subject

The first thing I would advise is that you teach a subject you are passionate about. You won't last very long if you dislike the subject you are teaching. That being said, there are particular specialties which can make you more employable and increase the likelihood that you will be promoted within a school. Take Science for instance. Here in New Zealand, biology specialists are pretty common, chemists are quite a bit rarer, and physics teachers are about the rarest of the bunch. Teaching a hard-to-staff subject can offer you protection from staff-reduction events (that may occur due to a decline in student enrollment) as a consequence of your ability to teach that specific subject.

Outside of the Sciences, other specialties that make you highly employable include mathematics, technology (think carpentry or metal-working), and languages (in New Zealand, that would be Te Reo (the language of the Maori) or in Canada—French). If you are in the planning stage and mapping out your courses before training as a teacher, email a few schools and ask which subjects are in demand and/or difficult to staff.

Choosing a school

"Make your mistakes at your first school, move on promotion to your next school."

These were the words of a colleague who I now recognize was an important mentor in my development as a teacher. You will make mistakes at your first school. Whether it be struggling with the behavior management of a class, mis-grading an assignment or two, or forgetting to fill out the correct paperwork for a field trip only to find out the night before; mistakes will be made. However, there will come a point when you have gained some proficiency in the day-to-day responsibilities of a teacher, at which point you might look for opportunities for promotion either within your current school or elsewhere. It is overwhelmingly likely that you will have to move schools to be promoted to a position such as a curriculum head/leader, assistant principal, deputy, or to the role of Principal. It is very rare that positions will become available within a school in a sequence that aligns with your professional readiness and preferred timeline. At some point, you will likely have to move to be promoted and progress in your career as a teacher. Therein lies both opportunity as well as a host of potential challenges, which will be discussed in greater detail in Lesson 26.

Each school is unique

Each school is unique. Even if you work within an educational environment in which the curriculum is quite prescriptive (as it is in the United States and the United Kingdom) and the structure of courses and their content is well-mapped, you will find that significant effort will have to be devoted in your new job to unit and lesson planning. After all, you may be assigned different year levels or grades to teach, or the school may have a particular emphasis on a specific mode of learning (e.g., inquiry learning). More likely than not, you will have to learn new procedures pertaining to student progress reporting and academic assessment. You will also have a brand-new network of colleagues. Perhaps most importantly, you will have new students. Arguably, the single most important variable that influences your success at a new school is how well you build relationships with your new students and the larger school community. Moving into a new school means starting from scratch in terms of building relationships with staff, students, and senior management. Combine that with the need to potentially teach and design new courses, units of work, and individual lessons and it is very much like rebooting your career each time you move schools. If you move on promotion, it means you typically take on a smaller teaching load in recognition of the management responsibilities you have. Having a management position also means that you have some control on how things are done within your sphere of influence (e.g., as a head of department, or the head of school-wide curriculum etc.). This means that to some extent, the system can adapt to your strengths rather than the other way round. Whether you decide to move on promotion or make a lateral change should involve careful consideration of the opportunities such moves entail with respect to your development as a teacher, weighed against the necessity to adapt to new school systems and to prepare resources for new courses you may teach.

LESSON 24: INTERVIEWS ARE LIKE FIRST DATES

When you arrive at a new school, you are quite probably a completely unknown variable. Don't be surprised that when applying for your first job or a regular classroom teaching role without management responsibilities, you are offered a fixed-term position. Unless you bring with you a long and uninterrupted history of distinguished service as a teacher, you may at first be viewed as a tentative addition to the school community. The reason for this is that teaching is a job that depends crucially on that most nebulous of concepts: *fit*. When searching for your first job as a teacher, you will attend interviews, which are intended to assess your fit with respect to a position and school.

One of my first interviews for a teaching position occurred at a medium-sized school in a rural New Zealand town. Though I didn't get the job, it proved to be one of the most instructive interviews I have ever had. At the time, I was fresh out of teacher's college and recently graduated from a PhD program where I had trained to be a research scientist. With no track record in high school teaching and only my educational track record and a few short-term jobs on my C.V., I was an unknown from the interview panel's perspective. Needless to say, the interview didn't go well. I later received a phone call from the principal of the school explaining why I didn't get the job—I was deemed to be too "academic." At first glance, you might be puzzled by that assessment. How is it possible to be "too academic" to teach at a school?

Truth be told, academic fit is almost an afterthought when it comes to working with adolescent students. You can have a PhD and be an awful teacher. Having an advanced degree can be a benefit to some extent; but at the end of the day, an advanced degree only means you know a bit about the academic corner you inhabited during your training. As I was to learn, the most important skill a teacher can possess is an ability to build productive relationships within the school community; and that means working effectively with students, parents/caregivers, and other teachers within the school.

The constructive advice I received at that first interview lit the proverbial fire under me. In my next interview at an even smaller rural school, I made a point of downplaying my academic track record and instead emphasized my enthusiasm for the subjects I could teach. I was successful in that interview and spent the next four years at a great little school in rural New Zealand. Was the Principal on the interview panel of that first school I interviewed at incorrect in their assessment? One could say "yes" and "no". Being fresh to the education job market, I didn't fully appreciate that the ability to build relationships is the most important skill a teacher can have. In hindsight, I didn't effectively demonstrate that I had that skill. So, in that sense, the principal was correct in his assessment and gave me really important feedback. Nevertheless, he was also incorrect in his assessment of my ability to build relationships. After all, I didn't have a personality transplant in the space of time between that interview and the next.

Interviews are like blind dates; you might know a bit about each other before meeting in person but really, it's first impressions during a face-to-face interview that count. So, give some serious thought to the manner in which you present yourself, as first impressions matter.

Interview panels will be looking for every reason to discount you. This is especially so if you are a "token" prospect/interviewee; i.e., someone who is interviewed out of necessity because the employer is legally required to entertain more than one prospect. For that reason, I would recommend that you assess your prospects by asking in advance why the position is being advertised (these are sometimes disclosed in the job advertisement anyway). Reasons a position might "actually" be vacant include:

1) The previous occupant of the position is departing the school on promotion or moving into a more senior position within the school.
2) A structural reorganization in the school's management/leadership structure is occurring, in which previous positions are disestablished and the previous occupants of the positions have to reapply for their jobs. In such situations, schools may be looking for "new blood" from the outside to execute strategic change.
3) A new department or curriculum area is being established.
4) There is significant roll growth (i.e., an increase in student numbers).

Internal candidates (i.e., people working within the school already) are sometimes favored for promotion to middle-management or senior positions, especially if there is no indication of roll growth to necessitate the addition of another staff member. Most often, advertisements entertaining outside prospects are sincere, but it is nevertheless worth working out what your chances are in the first place. Given how difficult it is to displace someone from a teaching position once they have been hired, a candidate who is known personally by the school or one of its members will always be on a firmer footing with the interview panel because they represent less of a risk. Nevertheless, even if you know your chances of landing a particular job are slim, it's worth going to interviews anyway to become more proficient in what is arguably a blind date.

The questions you could be asked in an interview

So, assuming you have been invited to an interview, what kinds of questions might you be asked when interviewing for a first-time position in teaching? Table 4 compares what you might be "asked" and what is potentially "meant" by those questions.

Table 4: Questions you could be asked during an interview for your first teaching job

What is asked	What is actually meant by the question
Tell us about yourself.	You are a complete unknown. Convince us that you're a relatively normal person.
Why did you become a teacher?	Convince us that you're not in the job for a pay cheque and the holidays.
A student asks if they can have your phone number so they can talk to you about an upcoming assignment that is due. What would you do?	We want to know if you understand boundaries and how to maintain professional relationships with students.
A student confides in you that they have been having suicidal thoughts. What would you do?	We want to know that you understand your limits as a classroom teacher and that you know when (and how) to share confidential information with

	the people in the school who are qualified to help with such situations.
As a teacher, how would you relate to someone of a different culture in your classroom?	We want to know that you're not a xenophobe and that you would acknowledge diversity in the classroom.
Imagine you have a new class and you have a range of learners, including gifted and exceptional students. How would you ensure that you are meeting their learning needs?	We want to know that you recognize that people are different and that you would make an attempt (including asking your colleagues for help when required) to adapt your teaching to their needs.
What strategies would you employ in your classroom to ensure that students are engaged in their learning?	We want to know that you will put some effort into lesson planning to pre-empt behavior management issues.
How would you describe your teaching style?	This is a variant of the previous question and is more likely to be asked at a school with a specific pedagogical philosophy (i.e., special philosophy of teaching and learning).
What is our school motto?	We want to know that you are applying to this school for a reason and not just throwing a dart at the map.
What would you do if you saw one of your colleagues	We want to know that you understand your professional

clearly mistreat a student?	responsibilities as a teacher and that you would communicate the issue promptly to a senior manager.
Consider a situation where you were driving a school van with some students in it on a field trip. While returning to school, one of your students leans out the window and gives the finger to a passerby. What would you do?	We want to know that you would do something / anything to correct the student's behavior, rectify the situation for the offended passerby, and protect the school's reputation.

Throughout the interview you can ask questions. Ensure that you have a list prepared as these not only reflect your level of interest in the school but also allow you to ask frank questions before you make the big decision about taking a position with a new school.

The types of managers you want to work for

I have had the good fortune of working for some exceptional managers while working in New Zealand schools. Typically, your line manager (who is the person you report to) will be your main point of contact within the school when you are looking for advice and guidance. For that reason, when you attend an interview your line manager will be on the interview panel (along with the principal or another member of senior management). In a large school, your line manager will likely be a head of faculty or head of department. If you are in a small school, you may report to the deputy or principal directly. In any case, it is worth finding out a bit about how each of these managers think and whether their management style is compatible with your approach to teaching. In my experience, the best managers are approachable and are willing to help you problem-solve, while still allowing you a significant degree of flexibility in how you run your classroom.

In an interview, asking general questions such as "What do you value?" and more specific questions such as "What do you expect in terms of student results and teacher performance?" allows you to gauge the degree of autonomy you are likely to have as a teacher in that school. What you require from management as a teacher will depend on a host of factors. If you are new to the profession, having a manager who helps you set defined targets and offers extensive guidance with regard to curriculum planning is probably beneficial. For instance, to assess the level of guidance you might have in your role you could ask to see an example of a curriculum map or plan for the subject you intend to teach. Table 5 outlines examples of questions you could ask during an interview to gauge the management style of the leaders at your school.

Table 5: Questions you could ask during an interview for a teaching position

What you could ask	What you are looking to find out
Why is this position being advertised?	Is this a new position created because of an increase in student numbers at the school? Did the person holding this job prior to you quit, or did they move on promotion?
What do you expect from your teachers?	This is purposefully vague; the purpose of this question is to find out a bit about your manager's style and approach to educational management.
How do you provide feedback to your staff on their development as teachers?	With this question, you are looking to find out how they conduct teacher appraisal / performance management.

Within your school, what does effective teaching look like?	Here you are trying to understand what your prospective manager values most. Is it exam results? Student engagement?
What kinds of opportunities for continuing training/ professional development do you provide for your teachers?	Is there a formalized system of professional development for staff?
What kind of support do you provide for new teachers?	This is important. You want to be assured that people new to the profession are given a mentor or some other form of structured support in their first years on the job.
Would I be able to take a tour of the school and speak to a few students?	Many schools will do this proactively.
How does the school support students in achieving their goals?	This is a deliberately broad question. It gives school management an opportunity to explain their vision for supporting student achievement.

One of the most valuable insights you can gain when interviewing for a teaching position is through a school tour and student interview. Table 6 outlines some questions you could ask students when touring a prospective school.

Table 6: Questions you could ask a student during a tour of a school

What you could ask	What you are looking to find out
What's your favorite part of the school?	What students value gives you an insight into points of difference that could set this school apart from others. For instance, does the school have a strong sporting history, trades training, or college/university preparation program?
What kinds of extracurricular activities are you involved in?	This will give you an idea of the range of extracurriculars on offer and how you might contribute to them? (Participation in an extracurricular club or sports is a requirement of almost all schools)
How do teachers support you in achieving your goals?	This is probably the most important question you can ask of a student. It gives you an idea of whether there is an overall vision or structure guiding student achievement across the school.

LESSON 25: DON'T GET COCKY!

Remember how in an earlier chapter I told you about a colleague who advised me that one should make their mistakes at their first school and move on promotion to their next? Well, that was advice I didn't heed and it nearly cost me my career.

I had started out as a teacher at a small rural school. About four years in, my wife took up a five-year training program at a university in another part of the country, which necessitated a move. It was a difficult decision to make, as I enjoyed working in that environment with a very supportive group of teachers and some great students. Nevertheless, there is more to life than your job and I wanted to be with my wife. Eventually, an equivalent full-time position teaching the same subject (Science) came up at a large co-ed school near the university my wife attended. I thoroughly enjoyed my time there; a couple of years in, I was given a promotion to be a Provisionally Certified Teacher Coordinator, whose job is to mentor beginning teachers. This was a rewarding job, as it allowed me to not only mentor some enthusiastic young people but also gain some new ideas and perspectives by observing them at work.

It wasn't long before my wife had graduated and she was looking for her first job in her field, which required another uplift and a move to a different part of the country. Truth be told, this time I wasn't as selective in choosing a school or a job. I was enjoying teaching, so what could be wrong with yet another change of scenery? Furthermore, my wife and I preferred not to work apart again, so hubris got the better of me—I jumped at the first job that came up in the town where my wife was going to work, this time at a medium-sized intermediate school.

Hubris

If there is one thing that can undermine your progress in any profession it is hubris. I had been working as a science teacher at my two previous schools before I took on the role of a Grade 8 homeroom teacher. Up to that point, things had been getting easier; with each successive year I had to devote less time to planning as I refined my units of work and database of teaching activities and resources. This meant that on a day-to-day basis, I could leave work at a reasonable hour. What's also important to note here is that when you can leave work at a sensible time, you have both the hours and the mental energy to have a life outside of work. This, as I soon discovered, was very important. When one asks teachers about the difficulties they face on the job, classroom and behavior management is one of the most consistent sources of stress reported. One of my colleagues described it best when he said that a significant source of fatigue for him is the "constant vigilance" associated with classroom management. Pre-empting, managing, and mediating conflict in the classroom is cognitively demanding; if your hours outside of work are also consumed with preparing lessons and communicating with parents, then you will have little time to recharge your batteries and have the energy to effectively manage a classroom. In addition to the workload associated with teaching a new year level and subjects, I also discovered that there were additional challenges associated with teaching a homeroom class for which I was unprepared.

Teaching homeroom vs. high school

In retrospect, I showed up to my new job as a homeroom Year 8 teacher with unwarranted confidence. One of the key distinctions between being a secondary teacher and a homeroom Year 8 teacher is in the configuration of the day and your contact time with individual students. As a secondary school teacher, you typically have a range of classes in a single day (think Year 9 Science followed by Year 12 Biology and so on...). As a homeroom teacher in a primary or intermediate school setting, that is generally not the case. In those situations, you will typically have the same group of students all day, every day (and you will instead teach a range of subjects to the same group of students). Herein lies both opportunity and a potential source of stress. If you're the type of person who likes routine in terms of having the same group of students all day, then homeroom teaching could be for you. However, if you like variety and the ability to have different classes in a single day, secondary teaching would likely be a better bet.

From my perspective, one of the significant advantages of teaching secondary school is that behavior management issues can be compartmentalized; that is, if you have a particularly challenging Year 9 class, you at least only have them for one hour a day. With homeroom teaching, that same class is with you, day in and day out. Do not underestimate how beneficial this can be to your mental well-being; if you have a cluster of challenging students in a homeroom class and you are the sole teacher for that group, you will be left with the challenge of managing them ALL DAY, EVERY DAY. In addition, the frequency of challenging behaviors tends to decline as students mature emotionally. Instead of managing challenging behaviors in senior classes (think Grade 11 and up), the sources of stress in senior classes typically center around the academic preparation of students for high-stakes examinations and college/university preparation. By teaching a mixture of age levels, the sources of stress become more varied instead of monotonous.

Another potential drawback of teaching a homeroom is that you are the sole point of contact with parents. Having previously worked in the private sector as an editor for a language services company and as a technical consultant for an agricultural outfit,

I was relatively well-versed in the essential skills of customer service. Just as you would find when working in a client-facing business, in education you will have to work with difficult customers. Let me be clear: most parents have their children's best interests at heart and sincerely want to work with you in helping their child achieve their potential. However, occasionally you will encounter parents who go about this in a misguided way and instead attempt to micromanage their child's life (and second-guess your management of their child's learning in the process). These are the so-called "helicopter parents" you may have heard about. As a secondary teacher teaching several classes, their attention on you as the teacher of a single subject among five or six others will be only a fraction of what it would be if you were instead the child's homeroom teacher. This is a significant point of difference between high school and primary/elementary teaching. Teachers increasingly report that they spend more of their time on emails outside of class time, as well as coping with parental expectations that they be available at night and on the weekend to respond to emails (this is not unique to teaching and is an issue in other industries as well).

Know yourself and your strengths

So back to hubris. Although I didn't know it at the time, when I accepted that job to work as a homeroom teacher, I was undertaking a vastly different job compared to that of a high school teacher. Furthermore, I was no longer teaching Science. Having trained as a scientist, I had forgotten how important my enthusiasm for the subject was with regard to being effective as a teacher. I have no doubt that for some people, the subject they teach is of secondary importance compared to their enthusiasm for mentoring young people in general. I suspect these are the sorts of people that make the best primary/elementary school teachers. The decision as to whether one should teach elementary versus secondary is a difficult one, as both can be quite rewarding. Table 7 outlines some questions you could ask yourself to help guide your decision-making.

Table 7: Questions you could ask yourself when deciding which year level / student age group you might want to teach, either when choosing a program of teacher education (secondary vs. primary) or when considering a teaching position in a new school

The question	What your answer might suggest
Are you a subject specialist, having studied one or more subjects to an advanced level at college/university? (e.g., did you major in mathematics or are you a trades/technical specialist etc.)	Consider secondary teaching, where you could spend time communicating your passion for specific subjects.
Do you want to teach a varied program of learning, which might involve teaching literacy, numeracy, physical education etc. to the same group of students?	In primary / homeroom teaching, you will teach a variety of subjects to the same group of students, so this could be a promising choice for you.
When you spend time creating resources for teaching (i.e., activities and tasks), do you have more fun creating activities for one subject in particular?	This might suggest you are more passionate about one particular subject than another. Teaching secondary school will give you the opportunity to devote more time to one subject.
Do you enjoy mentoring students as they "grow up"?	Consider primary/elementary teaching if you think you might enjoy the experience of

	mentoring a single group of students.

Having asked yourself some questions about where you might "fit" as a teacher, what happens if you find yourself in the wrong job?

Knowing when to call it quits

In changing jobs and accepting a position as a homeroom elementary teacher, I had failed to consider how important my passion for teaching science was in sustaining my energy and enthusiasm for the job. *Teaching itself was not enough.* As a Year 8 homeroom teacher, I found myself teaching everything from swimming to poetry. Although these things are important in their own right, I didn't find them meaningful (nor did I know much about how to teach them either). The stresses started adding up: the unfamiliar challenges of sustained classroom management in a homeroom teaching environment, the need to develop new resources and programs of learning for unfamiliar subjects, and the requirement to adapt to a new school and its systems. Week by week, I felt a little less enthusiastic about going to work. No doubt the students started to notice it too. By this point, I actively *disliked* my job, which is an odd place to be if you have enjoyed working with young people up to that point.

An unfortunate feedback loop soon took hold. First, I became less enthusiastic about being in the classroom; almost in lock-step the quality and extent of my lesson preparation and classroom management declined as well. By that point, I was spending the better part of the evenings and weekends ruminating on the requirements and anticipated problems of the upcoming week. I felt (and objectively was) out of my depth. Despite the assistance of some devoted and talented colleagues, I carried with me a nagging feeling that things were not going to get better. As the sources of stress compounded, it became clear that a change was required. So, I resigned.

After resigning, I took the opportunity to talk to a counselor about the stress I was feeling and the circumstances leading up to quitting my job. I would not hesitate in recommending the value of counseling when working through career troubles. Talking through your problems with someone *who does not know you* is enlightening. Too often, our expectations and perspectives are warped by the lenses we view the world through. Make no mistake, we all wear a special set of glasses to help us navigate the world we live in. That can be both a help and a hindrance, depending on the situation you find yourself in. In the end, the counselor helped me clarify what I valued and how I could ensure that the choices I made in the future were congruent with my interests and aptitudes.

I learned a number of personal lessons from this experience. First, it's okay to leave an untenable situation. When your gut tells you something isn't right, trust that instinct. I also learned that for me, teaching alone is not a sufficient reward; the subjects I teach mean something to me. *Meaning* can be a bulwark against adversity and an insulator against stress. Finally, as the old saying goes, "if it ain't broke, don't fix it." That's not to say don't try new things, just do so in a purposeful and considered manner. As Han

Solo said, "Don't get cocky!"

In the end, things came right. I quit that job, took some time off and moved back into the type of role I knew that I could add value in (as a secondary science teacher in a high school). Perhaps more importantly for those Year 8 students, by recognizing that homeroom teaching wasn't for me and leaving gracefully, I gave them the opportunity to have a teacher who was the "right fit" for their classroom.

CONCLUSION

Teaching is an unusual craft with unusual demands. In addition to "teaching," you may on any given day serve as mentor, coach, or counselor to students from any number of cultural and socioeconomic backgrounds. Despite the challenges and pressures of the job, you will be hard-pressed to find another career that offers such enduring prospects for finding both day-to-day and long-term meaning in your work. The Maori people of Aotearoa New Zealand have a proverb which encapsulates perfectly the source of meaning for a teacher:

He aha te mea nui o te ao

What is the most important thing in the world?

He tangata, he tangata, he tangata

It is the people, it is the people, it is the people

Money will not be the principal reward of the job. Nevertheless, if you choose your teaching subject and location of work purposefully, you will find yourself in the position of having rewarding and meaningful work. If you do your job well, over the course of your career you will have helped thousands of people in navigating some of their important life choices. For some of your students, your influence will be transformative.

What I want for you

Your first few years on the job will be critical in your development as a teacher. Make no mistake—those years will be challenging. The profession needs teachers who care about their work, their students, and their own well-being. You can't make a difference if you don't look after yourself. So, remember a few key points: do not try to do everything yourself, set realistic expectations for your performance, and finally, speak up and ask for help from your colleagues when you have a problem you cannot solve. Most importantly, remember that no job is worth sacrificing your health for; look for a better fit or take a break if you're getting worn down despite your best efforts. Lastly, listen to your colleagues. They represent the best source of advice and support during your initial years. The suggestions I have outlined in this book have been garnered from observations of other teachers' practice and the advice I have been given over more than a decade of teaching. I hope you will find this book useful as you get started in the profession. If you have any feedback or suggestions on the content of this book, please email me at jandrewwelsman@gmail.com.

www.ingramcontent.com/pod-product-compliance
Lightning Source LLC
Chambersburg PA
CBHW031923240526
45464CB00022B/671